$Praise$ for $Notes$

A crucial part of burnout management is social support - the act of being known by others, and feeling understood in what we face as mothers. Sometimes, when we struggle to find that support in-person, discovering camaraderie via print is our solace. *Motherland* reads like a diary of diverse stories, and mothers are sure to find themselves in the pages at some point along the way.

— JEN JOHNSON, PHD., BESTSELLING AUTHOR OF
THRIVING AFTER BURNOUT

Motherland is as real as it gets. I smiled, laughed and cried as all the chapters were so relatable and real. These women did not hold back any aspects of the journey of motherhood.

— ANGELA SOLOMON CHEMIST, ENTREPRENEUR
AND AUTHOR OF *WIN! FEAR IS NOT A FACTOR*

This beautiful collection is a brave and deeply intimate glimpse into the incredibly varied, challenging and rewarding experience of motherhood. I was very moved.

— MMI RICH, MARRIAGE AND FAMILY THERAPIST

Motherland is a beautiful compilation illustrating the depth of connection that is motherhood. Each story is unique and yet so profoundly relatable, I identified with them all. I felt a part of this circle of mothers as they shared their experiences and the lessons they learned through them.

— TERESA CRUZ FOLEY, AUTHOR OF *MINDFULLY INCLUSIVE: CONNECTING SOCIAL EMOTIONAL LEARNING WITH DIVERSITY, EQUITY, AND INCLUSION SKILLS*

Notes from

MOTHER
LAND ♡

*the wild adventure
of raising humans*

Notes From Motherland

THE WILD ADVENTURES OF RAISING HUMANS

RED THREAD BOOKS

Red Thread Publishing LLC. 2024

Write to **info@redthreadbooks.com** if you are interested in publishing with Red Thread Publishing. Learn more about publications or foreign rights acquisitions of our catalog of books: www.redthreadbooks.com

This book compilation is initiated by Sierra Melcher, the founder of Red Thread Publishing. If you would like to be published as an author in our future book compilations such as this please visit www.redthreadbooks.com or email us at info@redthreadbooks.com .

Paperback ISBN: 979-8-89294-002-3

Ebook ISBN: 979-8-89294-001-6

Cover Design: Red Thread Designs

The information and advice contained in this book are based upon the research and the personal and professional experiences of the authors. Some names and characteristics have been changed, some events have been compressed, and some dialogue has been recreated. Chapters reflect the authors' present recollections of experiences over time. The opinions herein are of each individual contributor. All writings are the property of individual contributors.

The publisher and authors are not responsible for any adverse effects or consequences resulting from the use of any of the suggestions, preparations, or procedures discussed in this book.

Dedication

*To everyone who has been a mother
and to everyone who has ever had a mother.*

Contents

Introduction   xiii

CHAPTER 1   1
Leaving the Nest
By Chris Chandler

CHAPTER 2   7
Mother Magic
By Sierra Melcher

CHAPTER 3   13
The Birth Plan
By JoEllen Irizarry

CHAPTER 4   23
Bad Mom (Or the Most Complicated)
By Jessica Goldmuntz Stokes

CHAPTER 5   33
...and...
By Brandee Melcher

CHAPTER 6   43
(Greatly) Modified Parenting Goals
By Jennifer Rhode

CHAPTER 7   49
Relationship Revival
By Reah Hagues

CHAPTER 8   59
Missing Children
By Sandi Phinney

CHAPTER 9   67
The BETTER Self Formula
By Erika Shalene Hull

CHAPTER 10   77
Momming with Luster 101: Reclaiming the Joy of Motherhood
By Ashley Wize

CHAPTER 11   87
Embracing the Haters and Helpers on the Journey to Motherhood
By Rena McDonald

CHAPTER 12   97
It Can't Have Landon
By Wendy and Sierra Riddle

CHAPTER 13   103
A Fitness Journey Through Time
By Audra Romeo

CHAPTER 14   113
Can't Fix It
By Frances Trejo-Lay

CHAPTER 15   125
The Stick & the Vine
By Sierra Melcher

Thank You   137
Acknowledgments   139
Other Red Thread Books   141
Red Thread Publishing   145

Publisher's Note

Dear Reader,

Welcome to *Notes from Motherland: Wild Adventures of Raising Humans*. Before embarking on this journey through the heartfelt stories within these pages, we wish to offer a prelude regarding the sensitive topics that are delicately explored.

This anthology is a tapestry of personal narratives, each woven with authenticity and vulnerability. Within these stories, you will find candid discussions about motherhood, womanhood, and the myriad of challenges and triumphs that accompany these roles.

Additionally, we want to acknowledge that some stories within this anthology contain themes of sexual violence, as well as stories of loss and illness of children. We understand that these topics can be triggering for some readers, and we advise discretion while reading.

We encourage you to approach these stories with an open heart and mind, knowing that each author's journey is a testament to the power of resilience, love, and the human spirit. Thank you for joining us on this poignant exploration of motherhood. May these stories resonate with you as deeply as they have with us.

With love,
Red Thread Publishing

Introduction

BY CHRIS CHANDLER

Motherhood is often sold to us as one picture: it's amazing and beautiful. It's airy and light and unicorns and rainbows. And it is those things. There is so much that is beautiful and rewarding. But it's a lot else too. It's that "else" that people often don't speak about. That leaves a lot of us feeling alone and strange and weird and not okay about ourselves as mothers. As if we are the only ones not living up to the vision.

The landscape of motherhood is as varied as the terrain of this earth. It is certainly the soaring heights and glorious sunsets from the summit. But it has its equal share of dry deserts and deep dark forests where trails (many of them unmarked) diverge, where it's easy to get lost at every turn. Crevasses are threatening to swallow you up, and no ropes are reaching the bottom. There are times when it seems like the map you have been handed is upside down or sideways. Or totally unrecognizable. There are times when it seems like you were handed a shiny brochure depicting the sunny beach, but when you're there, it has turned into a place with raging wind and waves beating the shore. You wonder if you failed to read the fine print on the back.

Did they offer travel insurance? Can you get your money back? Did you really mean to travel here? To a place like this?

There are many times I remember being 100% flummoxed. One of the first times was when I heard my younger son, about a year old at the time, upstairs in his crib awake from his nap. I walked into his room to find he had woken up and decided to finger paint. With the fresh poop from his diaper. There was poop **everywhere**—on him, the wall, the crib, the sheets. I opened the door, took one look at him, shut the door, walked out of the room, and called my mom. I had no idea where to even start. Another time was when my older son, then about eight years old, had to go to an appointment for a therapy he didn't like. He had been clear about his dislike, but it was something I felt he needed—even though it didn't seem to be working. I gave him the ten-minute warning that we'd be leaving for his appointment. When I went back upstairs to get him, he had locked himself in his room. I knew how to get the door unlocked, but what was I going to do? He was too big to grab into my arms and wrestle into a five-point car seat restraint.

My main thought at these times was that someone had ripped chapters out of my parenting manual. At that moment—and many to follow—I had absolutely no idea how to respond. How many times would I encounter situations with my kids where it seemed as if, metaphorically, there was shit smeared everywhere and I felt clueless?

This does not include any of the moments I felt blind rage, desperate fatigue, horror over a kid puking on my bed yet again (did you know that it's a milestone when your kid actually pukes into the toilet?!) And there were times I wondered what in the heck I was thinking when I decided becoming a parent was a good idea.

Don't get me started on adolescence. Most of what I thought I knew about teenagers, communication, and "good" parenting felt useless.

My master's degree in psychology with a focus on child development did not help. Nor did all the parenting books and "expert" advice.

Long before I had kids, a mentor of mine—someone I found to be wise and grounded, and who had two young kids—told me, "Kids will take you places you never knew were within you. Not all of it is good. They will take you from the heights of joy and ecstasy to the depths of blinding rage. And everything in between." I will never forget those words. And I have always been grateful for them because when I hit those moments in my parenting, the ones that felt confusing, maddening, surprising, or shameful, I thought back to them. They were confirmation that nothing was wrong with me but that I was on a mysterious, complicated journey with these other beings. And like on any challenging expedition, some days are better than others. Sometimes it is enough to just survive. Other days you will thrive.

The path through "MotherLand" is a journey, as individual as you are and as individual as each of the people you are mothering. There will be obstacles. There will not be perfection. There will be times when you will want to lie down on the trail and cry or yell or rave. And you will. There will be times you want to shout from the mountaintop with joy at the beauty of this connection, of this thing you are doing. There will be times you will be tempted to offer up your offspring to the next person who happens along the trail—or at least trade theirs for yours. At times, the way will feel too steep, and you will be certain you cannot make it to the top. On other days, the road will be easy, and the meadow will be full of wildflowers blooming. Sometimes the side of the hill will slump and avalanche down around you, pinning your hands. Sometimes you will successfully ford the stream, but your feet will get wet.

My hope for you is that this collection of essays about motherhood will leave you feeling like you have good company on the road—the company of other mothers offering up their adventures, their strategies, their doubts, their lessons, their sadness, and joys. May you, in their good company, feel held, seen, and understood. May you know you are not alone. You are doing just fine.

Chapter 1

LEAVING THE NEST
BY CHRIS CHANDLER

"Have you been dive-bombed by the hawk yet?"

The question comes from my neighbor, Larry, standing at the end of his driveway putting out his garbage cans.

"I have," he tells me, "and I have talon marks to prove it."

He points to the bike helmet on his head and explains that it is there not as preparation for a bike ride, as I had assumed, but as hawk protection. He goes on to list all the neighbors who have recently been given a clear message by the hawk parents: **too close, getaway!** The male and female birds fiercely protect their nest from predators like crows, raccoons, other falcons—and, apparently, people.

It's an intense undertaking to help these young hawks into the world. The female hawk stays on the nest almost exclusively for the thirty-four to thirty-six days it takes the eggs to incubate and then for another two weeks after the eggs hatch. The male hunts and brings food to her and the young birds.

In shooing people away from the nest, the defending hawk approaches from the back. My neighbors who have experienced it say there's no warning until you hear the rush of wings through the air and perhaps get a knock on the head. By then, well, it's too late.

On our neighborhood website, our local bird expert and neighbor explains that the hawk intends to scare you away from the area of the nest. "If you get dive-bombed, wave your hands or hat over your head until you're out of the area—and you're no longer getting attacked," he advises.

The nest, snuggled into a Y in the branches of a large Ponderosa pine in Larry's yard, is not far off the road that circles through the neighborhood. I'm tempted to stop as I walk by to try to see the babies and the nest, but it doesn't seem wise. Lingering in the vicinity is clearly not a good idea, so despite my curiosity and wonder, I keep moving.

The hatchlings emerge from their eggs with a short coat of fluffy, white-and-buff down. Over the next week or so, they develop a longer coat of thermal down, become able to regulate their own temperature, and start to move around the nest.

By week three, the young hawks have juvenile feathers on their wings and tail and have started to move beyond the nest, hopping onto branches, flapping their wings, and leaping at the tree trunk and small branches to practice grasping and balancing. The female continues to stand guard from a nearby branch.

At the same time, this hawk family is preparing to send three babies off into the world, my own chicks are spreading their wings. Soon they, too, will be fledging.

I feel a bit like the hawk mother right now, suddenly hyper-vigilant and over-wrought because my fledglings are perched precariously on the side of our nest, the last few downy feathers waving on their necks. In a month, we will load a van full of furniture and personal belongings, and drive our two sons plus their girlfriends 1,800 miles away. And leave them there. All on their own.

I'm uncertain what this flying thing will look like. Will there be immediate and easy soaring? Certainly, there will be growing pains as they become more independent. Except I will not be perched on the branch just above them to flap my wings and bare my talons at perceived predators.

One day our local bird expert and neighbor announces that the hawks have finally left the nest but are still in the area. The hawk parents have a few more weeks of feeding the young birds while teaching them to hunt on their own. I imagine it to be like our encouraging the kids to finish off the frozen pizzas in the freezer and take advantage of a few more home-cooked meals before they became totally responsible for procuring food and feeding themselves. Granted, the kids' task seems a bit easier than that of a young hawk zooming through the woods trying to catch small birds and other prey. But still.

And then comes the sad news that two of the young birds have been injured, both flying into windows. The birds are taken to the local birds-of-prey rehab center. The third seems to be faring well. When I tell my husband about the window bashing, he quips, "Well, the third, uninjured one is probably a girl." Indeed. Female Cooper's hawks are larger and tend to fledge a bit later. Having raised two boys with him, I have to laugh.

Of course, I wonder what form the window bashing might take with our own young flyers. It's an exciting time but also ripe with risk. I mean, does it really seem like a good idea to fling oneself into the air from high on a branch? And does it really seem like a good idea to drive your kids thousands of miles away, shove them out into their own apartment (after buying them dressers and decorating their bathrooms), and drive away? Why don't they start from lower down? Why aren't they starting out a tiny bit closer to home? Are my chicks launching from an optimal height?

As I anticipate their flight, my insides feel wobbly, and my appetite is questionable. I have a necklace with a charm on it that says, "Be Curious." It's a reminder of the way I want to approach life, especially when it gets challenging. But I feel like I am failing at this right now. Although I am trying to remain open about what this empty nest thing will look and feel like, mostly I am anxious and sad. When my husband and I arrive back home one day and both the kids' cars are gone while they are at work, he says, "See, in three weeks, this is how the driveway will look all the time—the new normal!" I am uncertain whether to cheer or cry.

There's a huge part of me that feels ready. Ready for me, ready for them. I'm ready to stop counting cars in the driveway and accounting for everyone's whereabouts. Ready to have my clean kitchen counter stay clean, to stop finding hiding places for the good towels and premium ice cream, and to not have to tell anyone to clean up their mess of discarded energy drink cans and wet bath towels. Did you know—actually, **of course** you know—that the mother bird keeps the nest tidy by removing shells and waste from the nest? That she eats any parts of the prey the young birds can't eat or digest, and she tidies up after each feeding? Alas, once they start self-feeding in the nest, it becomes littered with partly eaten prey—hence the term fouling the nest.

This is perhaps why I am fantasizing about having a dumpster delivered and throwing out half the contents of the house once they're gone. I've already told my husband to prepare himself to come home one day and find I've taken a box cutter to the nasty carpet in the kids' rooms and dragged it out into the garage.

And yet.

I can hardly remember what it was like to live in a house without kids. In the past few years, I haven't done a lot of caretaking for them, but their energy is in the house. And when they turn up in the afternoon after work or join us for dinner, or I hear the squeak of a bedroom door, I rest assured they are accounted for another day, my chicks still safely tucked into the nest.

My husband keeps saying to me, "It's going to be okay." I know he's right. I know that once I get through the transition itself, once I actually say goodbye to them, once I drive away and set out towards home, it will be fine. The question is how to make it through to that part. It's always hardest for me when I'm staring the object of my goodbye in the face.

And so, I have to make a plea to those around me. It goes like this: I'm sorry if I'm cranky like the hawks over the next few weeks. Please forgive me if I swoop down over your head squawking and beating my wings or if I bonk you in the noggin with my talons. My birdies will fly, I will feel less afraid, and I'll fly a little freer, too.

About the Author

Chris Chandler's life has been accurately summed up by the socks she has been gifted—ones that say "F*** off, I'm Reading," "Ringmaster of the Shit Show," and "All I Need Is My Dog." Plus a pair covered in avocados.

She is a storyteller, author, and book lover. Chris believes our stories are important. Why? Because through telling our stories we discover ourselves and our truths. When we offer our stories up to others, we connect, and we stop feeling so apart and strange and alone. By writing and sharing our stories, we heal ourselves and we heal the world—a quiet little revolution.

Much of Chris's writing centers on home, family, and parenthood. Her memoir, *Stay Sweet: Tales of Quirky Southern Love*, was published in May 2023 by Red Thread Books. She has been published on Scary-Mommy.com and in *The Boulder Magazine*. And she has found joy in telling her stories on stage at Boulder's *Listen to Your Mother* show and at the Boulder Story Collective She lives in Boulder, CO with her husband and too many animals. Her kids have flown the coop. She helps others find and tell their stories by facilitating writing circles for women. linktr.ee/chrischandler

Chapter 2

MOTHER MAGIC
BY SIERRA MELCHER

In the land of eternal spring, Medellin, Colombia, where the sun shines every month of the year and the people are all smiles, mother magic has found me.

In the quiet, near dark of early morning, a little voice calls from the foot of the bed. "Mas." She wants more. She is hungry. In the half-light, I reach for her. "Up" in a soft and delightfully pleading tone with it begs compliance. On tip-toes, both arms and one leg already on the bed, pulling the sheets tight and nearly able to climb up herself, she says again, "Up-mama." Her stuffed turtle with her always for comfort. She clings to its tag as I lift her into my enormous empty bed. A smile of triumph glows on her little face. Teeth, so many teeth in that little smile. "Mas," she says and signs, bringing her fingers together three times to make sure I understand.

She lets her head drop onto my chest. Soft cheeks brush my collarbone. The heavenly ecstasy of a motherly morning embrace. Her heavy body falling onto mine, without hesitation or resistance. A smile spreads across my whole body, and I sink into the moment. Nothing else could possibly ever matter. This is intoxicating divinity. "Uung, uunhh, unnn." She groans in that distinct, hungry-for-boob way, eager with anticipation and desperation. In any other context that sound would unquestioningly sound of sex, but she is hungry and as I pull up my shirt, she squeals and lets out a sigh as she dives in. Both of us relieved. She draws heavily on the nutrients in my breast and the growing pressure in me subsides. We breathe together in a slow comfortable rhythm.

The trust and routine make this morning blend in with hundreds before it; on this morning, my mind wanders into the future and recognizes the preciousness of these fleeting moments. She has only been sleeping in her own bed for a few weeks: *She is growing so fast. How many more times will I get to wake up to such a precious greeting? Someday soon, we will be in a rush, off to school and work or just growing up and wanting different things, wanting more than to snuggle in momma's arms. How could I ever want anything more than this? I couldn't. But I know soon she will transition into yet another phase and be a slightly bigger girl, increment by increment until she is grown and we will never snuggle.*

And then she bites me a little too hard, and I am immediately brought back into the moment. No time to mourn the future or romanticize the present. My startled look meets her startled and slightly mischievous gaze. A half smile in her blue-gray eyes. She waits almost as if to see my next move. Time waits. The world shrinks to the space between our faces. She breaks the tension. "Get down. Ekk," she says as she rolls and slides down the side of the bed tottering off towards the kitchen. She wants an egg. And so the morning becomes far too real. Hardly 6 am; too early to cook, let alone stand up. I commit. Feet are on the ground. This is happening. No hope of a few more minutes.

"Ekk" she beckons. Dressed or half-dressed I slide into my slippers because the tile floor is brutally hard. I scuff towards the kitchen longing for one more minute of horizontal snuggles, but the day wins. Eden wins; she is hungry.

The light of the day greets me and entices me to smile and take a deep breath. There is no hurry and it is gorgeous out already. Is it December or May? Not sure. They are all the same. I love the tropics.

Cool fresh sunshine pours in the front window and the birds are arguing harmoniously about something out in the trees.

"Mamma, up. Doodeli." Looks like we are having blueberries for breakfast while the egg cooks.

Thank goodness for the frozen blueberries from the import store. Life in a foreign land certainly has its perks. There are a few things we have to fight for. Here, frozen blueberries are a cherished treasure.

She stuffs one in her mouth and chews. A look of sincere concentration on her face as if tasting this for the first time. Cold. Sweet. Hard, yet chewy. Her eyebrows come together. A look of consternation as if she's made a bad choice. Then delight. All her teeth showing blue goop as her smile dashes across her face. Another, yes. Covered in blue purple smears she holds one out to me and I lean in as she feeds me. "Nom, nom, nom." I gobble her hand and the berry too. She squeals with delight and immediately thrusts another berry in my direction. We repeat this game until there are no berries left, just the blueberry warpaint on her cheeks, shoulders, pajamas, and my left arm. We are ready for our day.

There is no rush. Still no school or *guarderia* to cart her off to. No job to rush off to. We live in the yoga studio I run. While she naps, when she naps, I get something done or try. She has hours of exploring before she is ready to crash this morning. So the day lies ahead of us. Full of moments to explore new things, practice new words, and totter.

New clothes, socks and shoes. Chubby little thighs hanging out of cute ruffles. My girly-girl daughter. I would never have imagined, dripping in pink and polka dots. Striped socks, pink suede, dirt-scuffed high tops. The things people buy for babies. I don't look nearly as well put together, but I also believe I'll never have sex again, so what does it matter?

We emerge into the light of the street and repeat the game to find what we can climb. The steps of the building down the street are a current favorite. The unimaginable joy of climbing up these seven steps just to climb down again.

And again, and again.

She is my teacher. Teaching me the magic of motherhood. The simplicity of the moment, of every moment. Whether we are climbing, eating, snuggling, bathing, or crying. It just is. There is no before and there is no after; there is just the moment. She is my little Buddha master. I am a dedicated student, but not... what is the word? The mind of a mother is constant and striving. What is the WORD? Just on the tip, well, not the tip of my tongue. Really, it is in a pile with some other stuff I haven't used in a while in the back right recesses of my mind, like my closet. The point being that I am no great student. Persistent, attentive, but not yet there. Not getting every lesson or opportunity to be present. Maybe when I'm half asleep, I am there savoring every moment. But often I drift forward or back. *What will it be like when she's older? What should I say if her father shows up? Did I do the right thing? Will we live in Colombia forever?*

"Boom" WHAT? I am back in the moment. She tripped and is down. I am needed. I pick her up and brush her off. She is tough and is right at it again. Does she need me or do I need her? Yes. My little teacher pulls me back to the now. The lessons of mama magic are subtle, innumerable, and constant. Nothing special and everything miraculous. Everything is both work and play. Learning for us both as we grow up into a family. As we become the people we will be. She becomes this person to be known as Eden, and I am growing into a mother-version of myself. We are a little team. A living, loving mother-daughter team. Teaching each other as we go.

Expats in a foreign land like guests or tourists in a home that will never be entirely ours, for better and worse. Visitors. Making each moment even more unique. As a foreigner, everything seems odd already, heightening the preciousness of the moment. Hand-in-hand. Tottering down the foreign street, our street. A little wobbly and slightly out of place, in this familiar home we made out of nothing; this family we have made out of nothing.

The balance comes from our connection. Sometimes we each fall. Still learning as we go. And when we do we are there to brush each other off and keep on.

Mother magic keeps every moment special, even the monotonous because we do it together.

*Originally published in *Single Mothers Speak on Patriarchy*, Girl God Books 2016. Reprinted with permission.

Chapter 3

THE BIRTH PLAN
BY JOELLEN IRIZARRY

I n October of 2010, I peed on a stick and it turned blue, changing my life forever.

I had never really thought about having kids. It just felt like something society expected from women: you grow up, you get married, you start a family. Coming of age in the 1980s, all the women I knew had children, except for the eccentric art teacher who lived with her female "life friend" on the outskirts of town. It was not that I did not want children, it just was not a priority. I was married, working as a nurse, and traveling whenever I could. The idea of having babies could wait until later in life.

In the summer of 2010, I spent a month in rural Kenya volunteering in health clinics, primarily focusing on women and babies. The local women arrived at the clinics on foot, carrying their little ones snugly strapped to their bodies with colorful cloths known as kangas. I watched as the women would remove their babies, who were always naked except for a red string tied around their bellies ("for protection!" the women would say), and hold them in the air to let the baby urinate and defecate into the dirt outside of the clinic before wrapping them back up again. I could not believe that they had essentially potty-trained their infants. I became fascinated by how the women cared for their babies without all the modern conveniences people had back home. As I spent more and more time with them, something stirred deep within me. For the first time in my life, I felt an undeniable yearning for a baby of my own.

When I returned home, I threw away my birth-control pills and announced that I wanted a baby. My husband, accustomed to my spontaneous impulses, good-naturedly went along with my plans to become pregnant, expecting that I would change my mind once the initial excitement wore off. After all, I was thirty-three years old and had been on birth control since I was eighteen—it was not like I would get pregnant overnight. I figured I had plenty of time to reconsider if I wanted to.

A month later I was pregnant.

As I stared at the blue stick, I was filled with a mixture of excitement and terror. I wondered if I was ready for this—could I handle motherhood? Placing my hand on my still flat stomach, I could not help but smile. I imagined a spirited little girl, a mischievous blond child, a mini version of myself. My mother always joked that I was an "awful baby" who "never slept," and now I chuckled thinking of the tiny baby growing inside me. "Bring it on," I whispered to her, "I am ready for you."

As my stomach grew, I became more and more interested in the idea of natural childbirth. I recalled a scene from my travels in the Ecuadorian rainforest when a medicine woman demonstrated how the local indigenous women gave birth standing up, clutching a rope, while their partners held and supported them from behind. This practice, known as "vertical birthing," has endured for centuries. Modern research supported its benefits, suggesting it aided the baby's passage through the birth canal. Remembering this, I delved deeper into natural birthing methods, devouring books written by midwives on home births and watching videos of women laboring in birthing pools. I enlisted the support of a doula, a trained companion who offered emotional and physical guidance during labor. I spent hours planning out my "perfect birthing experience" —at home; on my own terms; with only my doula, midwife, and husband by my side. I longed for the primal essence of childbirth—the pain, the blood, the raw intensity that transcends time and cultures. I wanted to experience each contraction as my body gradually opened, releasing my baby into the world. I envisioned the moment my newborn would be placed on my bare chest, still coated with the remnants of birth, guided by instinct to seek nourishment from my milk-engorged breasts. I longed to embrace this profound journey from Woman to Mother.

I became obsessed.

Doctors and hospitals became the enemy. I joined online natural childbirth communities where any deviation from the "natural" path —like opting for formula feeding, having a C-section, or requesting pain medication—was met with ridicule and scorn. I took classes in natural childbirth, sitting in circles with other pregnant women, all of us connected by the lives growing inside of us, inhaling and exhaling in tandem, and learning how to breathe through the pain. I listened to guided meditations to strengthen my mind, dabbed lavender oil on my wrists to relax my body, and massaged my perineum with oils to prevent tears. In my mind, I was a natural goddess channeling the ancient magic of creating life! I was determined to embrace a natural, intervention-free birth as women had done for thousands of years. I had it planned out perfectly.

My body, however, had other plans.

During my second trimester, I developed high blood pressure, which prompted my midwife to refer me to an OB/GYN doctor. Reluctantly, I went and was taken aback by how different the experience was. Visits with my midwife were always calm and unhurried; the OB/GYN, however, was cold and detached. He diagnosed me with gestational hypertension almost in passing, barely giving me a chance to speak before handing me a prescription and moving on to the next patient. Feeling overwhelmed, I did not have the chance to ask questions or voice my concerns.

Seeking guidance from my online group, I hesitated to mention the prescribed medication, fearing their judgment. When I told them about the diagnosis, they recommended lavender oil and guided meditation. I followed their advice but also took the pills without telling them, ashamed of needing them. At first, my blood pressure stabilized, but soon it began to rise again. Despite higher doses of blood pressure medications, it continued to climb until I was sent to the hospital for observation. Suddenly, I was labeled a "high-risk pregnancy" and everything fell apart.

I was sent to a perinatologist, who made me collect my urine into a large plastic container and then lug it into his office for analysis. He increased my medications, put me on bed rest, and informed me I would need to be induced at thirty-seven weeks. He represented everything I had worked so hard to avoid. The only positive thing was the weekly ultrasounds done to monitor my baby's growth; I loved to watch my baby moving and kicking on the screen as the tech glided the ultrasound wand over my belly. We found out we were having a boy, a surprise as I had envisioned a girl throughout my pregnancy. "My son," I would whisper in awe, as I watched the blurry image move around on the screen.

Despite the joy of the ultrasounds, I remained frustrated with my body for not cooperating with my plans. I continued prenatal yoga, acupuncture, and meditation, hoping my body would respond, but my blood pressure remained stubbornly high. The doctors repeatedly urged me to consider early delivery, even suggesting a Caesarian section at thirty-seven weeks. I was horrified—there was no way they were going to cut me open and remove my still-growing baby! They finally insisted that I be induced at thirty-nine weeks, and I reluctantly agreed under the condition that I could proceed with a natural birth in the hospital, supported by my trusted midwife and doula.

With a week to go before my scheduled induction date, I was secretly determined to go into labor naturally before my induction date so I would not need to be induced. I scoured the internet for tips to induce labor, trying every suggestion: I ate spicy foods, bounced on an exercise ball, walked upstairs, tweaked my nipples, drank red-raspberry-leaf tea, had sex with my husband, went for extra acupuncture treatments, and had a prenatal massage. Nothing worked. Despite all my efforts, I did not go into labor on my own and had to be admitted to the hospital to be induced.

As they fastened the hospital bracelet around my wrist, I wanted to cry. The nurse administered medication to help "open and ripen" my cervix in preparation to be induced the next morning. They told my husband to go home and get some sleep because I likely would not go into labor until the following day; however, at 4:00 a.m., I awoke suddenly to a painful pressure in my pelvis and a strange urge to get out of bed and walk. The nurse came in and, sure enough, I was in labor. Ecstatic, I paced the hospital halls for hours, pausing to breathe through each contraction, and relishing this time alone with my thoughts. I felt empowered and optimistic, convinced that I could deliver this baby without further medical intervention.

At 8:00 a.m., my midwife arrived to check my progress and announced that I was four centimeters dilated and completely effaced. I continued to labor happily with my doula and my husband at my side. "This is not so bad," I reassured myself, "I can do this!" My contractions started getting stronger and faster, and I hoped I was close to delivery. When my midwife checked my progress, I was certain she would tell me I was ready to push. Instead, she revealed that I was still only four centimeters dilated. I was shocked. I could not believe that I had worked so hard without making any progress. I became angry at the doctors for forcing me into labor, angry at my body for not cooperating, and angry at myself for agreeing to come to the hospital at all. Though my midwife offered to break my water, I stubbornly refused, determined to do it on my own.

As the hours dragged on, my contractions intensified, one starting before the last finished, giving me no break, no reprieve, just constant, body-wrenching pain. I started to moan, sounding more like a wounded animal than a human. I felt like I was losing my mind —all I remember is raw, hot, constant pain and the worried look on my husband's face. At 6:00 p.m., I begged my midwife to check my progress, certain that after hours of painful contractions, I was getting close to delivery. Her face fell as she reached inside of me—I was stuck at four centimeters. I had labored for ten hours without making any progress. The nurse checked my blood pressure and it was dangerously high. I was becoming weak and delirious with pain. My midwife strongly suggested an epidural, telling me that I needed to rest. I gave in.

The nurse instructed me to remain perfectly still while they started the epidural, despite the constant contractions wracking my body. They would not let my doula or husband near me while the doctor prepared to insert the large needle into my spine. The nurse helped me sit on the side of the bed and then wrapped her arms around me and held me tightly in a bear hug. She told me to drop my shoulders and curve out my back "like an angry cat." She gripped me tightly and murmured soft words as the doctor worked behind me. I felt intense pressure and heard a loud crunching sound as the needle was pushed into my back. An electric shock ran down my legs and then, suddenly, the pain was gone.

With the nurse's assistance, I eased back into the bed, laying there in stunned silence. After hours of pain, I now felt nothing. As my mind cleared, I was finally able to process what had happened, and a wave of regret and shame washed over me. I had given up. I had failed. If I could not endure natural childbirth, how would I handle the challenges of motherhood?

Suddenly, my thoughts were interrupted by a gush of wetness— my water had broken. An hour later, I was surrounded by my midwife, doula, and husband and ready to push. With each push, my son's head would appear and then disappear, emerging and then retreating. At one point, I reached down and touched his soft strands of hair for the first time. It felt surreal.

Soon, my baby's head came out halfway and did not go back in. With my next push out came his head and then his shoulders; the midwife told my husband to "reach under the baby's arms and pull him out." After a brief moment of hesitation, he reached down and helped guide our baby into the world. The midwife took him and placed him, still covered in fluids and blood, onto my bare chest. He blindly moved his head and tiny hands, seeming to pound my breast. I watched in anticipation to see if he would root for my nipple, as I had read newborns would do, when the nurse whisked him away to "keep him warm." The moment shattered, I looked around and realized I was still in a hospital bed, attached to an IV, numb below the waist, and my baby was taken to the nursery to be weighed and cleaned. My midwife told me I had tears in my perineum (so much for time spent applying oils and stretching the skin), but since I was still numb from the epidural, I could not feel her stitching me back together. I laid back and closed my eyes and heard a voice inside of my head.

You failed.

All my research and planning, just to end up here, powerless in a hospital bed. This was not how it was supposed to happen. What was I going to tell my online natural childbirth group? I was ashamed of my weakness, of my inability to bring my child into the world without medical intervention. My own mother had delivered me in less than five hours—"You came too quickly for pain meds!" she said. What was wrong with me?

Though I should have been grateful to have had a healthy baby, all I could feel was a sense of failure. Months of immersion in the natural childbirth community had brainwashed me into thinking there was only one "right" way to give birth, and anything else was a failure. Exhausted and ashamed, I thought that at least now that he was born, I could return to my carefully laid plans. Surely, everything would be better moving forward!

Then, I tried to breastfeed.

I awoke to the sound of my baby crying as the nurse wheeled him in for a feeding. I undid the top of my hospital gown and reached for him, confident in my preparation from childbirth class that I knew how to position myself and the baby. He was crying, mouth wide open, and I guided him to my breast, feeling his warm mouth on my nipple, and then...nothing. He was still crying. I tried again...nothing. I squeezed my nipple gently, causing a few drops of warm, white liquid to fall onto his lips hoping it would cue him that it was time to feed, but no matter what I did, I could not get him to latch onto my nipple.

I looked up at the nurse and started to ask for help, but she just sighed deeply and said "Give him a bottle and try again tomorrow." I jerked back as if she had slapped me. A bottle! And formula? I was not going to allow my baby's first meal to be formula. I tried again with my other breast without success. I asked her if there was anyone who could help me, and she said the lactation consultant would not be there until the morning. The baby was crying louder, and I was getting frustrated. My breasts hurt, but the baby could not seem to figure it out. I turned to the nurse and said, "What can I do?" and she handed me a tiny bottle of formula and said, "Problem solved." and walked out of the room. Left alone, tired, and overwhelmed, I continued to try to breastfeed, but after several attempts gave up and gave him the bottle.

I wish I could say that bringing my baby home helped to alleviate my feelings of failure and shame, but they hung over me like dark clouds for months. Every time I heard about someone giving birth at home or watched as a woman effortlessly breastfed their baby, I felt ashamed. I withdrew from the online mother's group—I felt I no longer belonged there. When I returned to work, I tried to pump, but as a nurse working in a busy hospital, it was impossible to find the time. Reluctantly, I relied more and more on formula. I started going to therapy, as I was afraid that I had postpartum depression. My therapist thought my attempts to have the "perfect birth" were based on a deeper fear of becoming a mother and relinquishing my former control over my life. "But I can't even breastfeed!" I would wail. "It's ok," my therapist responded, "I never breastfed my children." I refused to see her again.

Several months later, something happened that would change my perspective on motherhood in a profound way. Unfortunately, this revelation arrived in the form of a devastating tragedy suffered by a close friend and fellow new mother. She lost her infant son who had gone into the hospital and not survived emergency surgery. My heart broke for her, and, as I cradled my own precious baby, I realized how foolish I had been. My baby was safe, happy, and healthy, and that was all that mattered. Motherhood was going to be full of challenges and imperfections; I was going to make mistakes and that was okay. I looked down at my baby happily drinking formula from a bottle and I smiled—my transition into motherhood was a success.

About the Author

JoEllen Irizarry was raised in a small town in western New York (Go Bills!) and moved to Tampa, Florida to attend college in 1996. She received a BA in English from The University of Tampa and worked as a technical writer before returning to school to become a registered nurse in 2008.

JoEllen loves to travel and has visited over twenty countries as a solo traveler. She feels that traveling solo has made her a more confident, open-minded, and resourceful woman and encourages other women to explore the world whenever possible. JoEllen has also spent time in Ecuador on a nursing study abroad program in 2008, and in rural Kenya as a volunteer nurse in 2010.

JoEllen lives in Tampa, FL with her husband and son. When not working or traveling, JoEllen loves to paddleboard in the ocean, curl up with a good book, and write about her adventures.

linktr.ee/jotravelssolo

Chapter 4

BAD MOM (OR THE MOST COMPLICATED)
BY JESSICA GOLDMUNTZ STOKES

I am not sure when the first time the nasty voice in my head whispered, *"You are a bad mom."* It is incessant and irrational, and it feeds ambivalence and doubt in me.

I do, however, know the first memories I have related to motherhood. They are not even my own, but a memory with my mom.

I had this cat, Maria, who let me dress her up in doll clothes. I was pushing her around in my baby stroller. I loved imitating Mom. My brother was playing with cars in the dirt. Or at least, I think that is what he was doing.

 What would you both think if you had a baby brother or sister?" Mom asked off-handedly as if to suggest, "Maybe... someday..." I imagine her hand was holding her belly.

I must have been about six, my brother, four. We were playing outside our house. It must have been one of those warm Colorado winter sunshine days. The grass was not in full bloom, but rather still dry and dormant.

I remember thinking that sounded wonderful. I liked being an older sister. Another baby! That would be fun! Then I also realized I would have to share my mom even

more. Even my young self knew this would be hard. I loved
all the attention I got from Mom.

Years later, I would discover that in and around this memory, Mom did get pregnant and had an abortion. Not once, but twice. It was the late 70s and abortion was legal. Mom and I would unravel this over the years. She would let me into some of her feelings about this time in her life. She wanted more kids. She thought Dad did not. There were lots of reasons for their decision-making. Mom never told Dad how much she really wanted more kids. Dad was more direct in his desires of a small family. He says now that he would have done anything Mom had wanted. At the time, Mom was not able to assert herself and share her wants about this with Dad.

I am not sure Mom was ever comfortable with the decisions she made. In fact, I think it followed her for the rest of her life. She made the choices, partly for Dad, and in direct discord with herself. However, it gave her the resolve to be the best and most devoted mother to us, and she was. I think she always felt guilty, and a little bit sad. *Maybe she felt like a bad mom.* She buried this guilt and sadness. I think she maybe hid from it. It became her secret.

Then it became my secret. Mom shared with me her experiences when I was twenty. I was in college, and marveling at my own processing of my abortion. I was basking in connection with other women and sharing our experiences, so different from Mom's experience. Then again, everything about my experience was different than Mom's.

I was seventeen the first time I got pregnant. I wasn't ready. I had a pretty clear trajectory of my life that did not include teen pregnancy. There is no judgment; I just didn't want it. I knew what my decision was. There were no questions about what I would do. I never entertained having a baby then. I never discussed this option with my boyfriend. I am grateful I had the emotional conviction that I was able to choose this for myself. I am extra grateful I had the support of my parents and the money to pay for it, and my boyfriend didn't hate me, or force me to do anything other than what I wanted.

All these years later, I also feel guilt. Guilt about privilege. Guilt about my choices. Guilt about my body. Maybe I just absorbed my mom's guilt. Perhaps this is when I first felt like a bad mom.

I found a women's health clinic that was housed in a converted old, two-story Victorian house. On the day of my abortion, Mom, Dad, and my boyfriend waited in the lobby for me. Walking down the rickety non-ADA-approved stairs to the waiting room was hell. All the hormones coursing through me, the emotions of sadness and relief that I didn't know how to process were overwhelming and heavy in my body and soul.

I knew my decision and I never questioned it. Why was I still feeling these feelings? I was not paying attention or even aware of the hormone surge that happens during pregnancy.

In hindsight, the day of my abortion and my experience in, and around it, were amazing. The three people that mattered to me most were all there. Waiting for me. Loving me. Not judging me. Not all young women are blessed by this kind of support. Not all states allow this kind of women's health center to exist. Not all people believe women have the right to this type of choice.

Can you imagine what it must have been like? When I put myself in the shoes of Mom, Dad, and my boyfriend in that waiting room that day, I was in awe.

Mom must have been feeling so many things. Years later, when I asked her why she never told me in real time about her own journey, she said she didn't want to take my own experience away from me. It must not have been easy, watching your daughter choose something that she had her own conflicted feelings about. While I was so clear on my choice, Mom had a deep unresolved conflict. I didn't want to have a baby. She did. I wonder if she felt like she had failed me.

Dad was wonderfully supportive of me. At the time, I just felt loved by my dad. Now, I wonder if it was also his way of supporting Mom and those long-ago decisions they made.

My boyfriend? Well, that must have sucked.

I always wanted to be a mom. I never questioned it. Perhaps I wanted to be like my mom: exceptional at motherhood. I wanted to be a wife, too. All other aspects of my life, I knew I would figure out. But those roles—mom and wife—were part of my destiny.

As I grieved and processed my abortion, a new *knowing* started to bloom in my body. At seventeen, this destiny took on a new shape. Viscerally, deep in my body, I knew the feeling of life inside of me. I didn't want it when I felt so much like a child myself, but I also *desired it*. I knew what it felt like. I knew I would feel it again.

I also knew I would have two children: a boy and a girl.

I would become a mother at age twenty-nine when I gave birth to my son. And sixteen months later I would have my girl. I now had my boy and my girl.

From the start, it was not an easy ride. Nothing about motherhood came naturally to me. I had high expectations. I expected I would be great at motherhood, but I wasn't.

Pregnancy was the exception. I loved being pregnant. All three of my pregnancies (yes, even the one I terminated) taught me lessons. My pregnancy with Hannah, the third, gifted me the best lessons. I relaxed into it. My body knew what it was doing. It built a deep intimacy and bond with her, one that I felt from the moment I conceived and I still feel to this day.

My body failed me at the birthing phase. I wanted the birth to be amazing. I imagined a natural birth with no complications. My body behaved differently. With my son, Abe, I never dilated. I labored for what seemed like forever. Dad did hypnosis, a skill he used with his patients in his psychiatric practice and Mom did Therapeutic Touch (energy work) she practiced as a nurse. My massage therapist friend joined us, too. The day was magic, but I never did get past eight centimeters.

My natural birth plan was truly thwarted when Abe turned around in my belly and got tired. I tried to forgo the pain-medicine cocktail, but wow—that epidural was amazing! Abe was an emergency C-section birth. I was forced to let go of expectations of what I had planned.

My daughter, Hannah, was an elected C-section. I had hoped it would set my body up for success for breastfeeding. Not so much.

Breastfeeding. Fail. Not once, but twice. My milk never let down. I never knew that feeling that so many women had. I yearned for that. I wanted to breastfeed my babies well past when it was acceptable. I was **that** mom, but alas...fail. No milk. Seriously. None.

Aren't we made for this? Isn't my womanly body supposed to know what to do? My body, apparently, did not. Was this punishment? I stopped the process at seventeen; at twenty-nine, was this my burden to bear? In stopping that pregnancy, was the universe punishing me?

That *knowing* I felt so strongly twelve years earlier...was it in error? I was still going to be a mom. Of two children. A girl and a boy. That *knowing* never changed, but this heavy-duty lifting of motherhood was just not natural to me at all. Wasn't I supposed to be good at this?

The mom thing was supposed to come easy. The other stuff was going to be what I "figured out." I had always been good at achieving. I am absurdly good at it. I never thought motherhood would be any different than other aspects of my life.

When my daughter, Hannah, was born, the kids' dad and I were navigating the crumbling of our marriage. Just six weeks after she was born, Peter moved out.

Not only was motherhood hard for me, but apparently marriage was, too. I thought I would be better at these roles. I just kept feeling as if I was failing. Maybe this is when that nasty voice reminded me, *"Good moms don't divorce the dad. You are not natural at this. You are failing."*

The voice became louder as Peter and I navigated our divorce. The voice was juxtaposed with a fierce mama-bear protection that rose up. I was going to protect these babies no matter what.

Our lives became complicated. Two children, so close in age, two households, and despite our desires to make the rules similar, there were two sets of rules. We did our best. Or tried. Besides shared parenthood responsibilities, I was working full-time and learning how to run my household solo. A huge zinger that I did not know yet was that my mom's Alzheimer's diagnosis was in the very near future. This would change everything about our lives.

I have memories from my children's childhood that I can't define which child they match with. I have deep regret about this. I am sad for them and me.

No wonder that *"Bad Mom"* voice took hold.

The whispering voice was not rational. Intellectually I *knew* I was not a bad mom, but that incessant nasty voice was hard to reckon with, and it was hard to ignore.

It seemed Peter, their dad, was a better mom than I was. He was very good with them, especially when our children were young. He can play with kids better than anyone I know. It was intimidating to be a parent in partnership with him. I don't think he has any idea how intimidated I was by him, and I am grateful. Not all ex-wives feel the way I feel about my ex-husband. He has been a good father to our children. He was patient, kind, thoughtful and playful. He delivered in the dad department.

Perhaps I should show myself the same amount of grace that I extend to Peter.

Being a mom is the hardest thing I have ever done. It is also the best thing I have ever done. It has pushed me to my limits and taught me so many lessons.

In an alternate universe, I am not sure I would choose to be a mother. Don't get me wrong: I love my kids and I love being their mom. If I had to do it over, I don't know if I would- but I did, and I love that I did.

That voice. Nasty and judgmental and laced with untruths.

How come I felt like I failed at motherhood?

If I am totally honest with myself, I didn't fail at all.

At times, I did not give my kids the full focus and attention they deserved. I was distracted by my life. I justified it by telling myself that I was leading by example—they would learn from my actions by watching me and they did learn.

There were years when they both hated me and I kind of hated them. But, oh, my goodness, most of the years (even those I hated them), I also loved them so much. The love I have for my children transcends words. There *are* no words. The visceral feeling of motherhood and being their mom is greater than any other thing in my life. It is the *knowing* I sensed when I was seventeen. It is more than I can even articulate. It is the sun and the moon. The darkness and the light. It is deep in my heart and all my being. It is cellular. It is my DNA, visceral and mercurial. It is everything.

I would become better at motherhood, but it would take a while. I relaxed and stopped getting caught in my own expectations. Perhaps I slowed down and was able to observe myself more. Maybe I became a better mother, as I was losing my mom to Alzheimer's. In navigating our journey and understanding her illness, I was able to also see myself and my role differently.

*Maybe I am **not** a bad mom.......*

My kids are now twenty-one and twenty-two. They are incredible humans. I am sometimes in awe that I birthed them. That I grew them in my belly. Perhaps all moms say this, but seriously, it is freaking amazing that we can grow people, and they are amazing people.

Not only do I love my children, but I also *like* them. They are lovely human beings. They both know the importance and necessity of mental health and a healthy touch. They give great hugs and know their boundaries. They are extraordinary humans. They both have a deep desire to explore and know their own truth. They are smart, kind, and gentle people who respect others.

So, what is that feeling that I was a bad mom? On the contrary, like so many of us, I did the best I could. I love them deeply. I see them for who they are. I love who they are. I love that they both know themselves.

Is it society? Do all of us mothers feel like we are not good enough? Is it my own judgment of myself? Do I feel guilty about divorce so young in my children's life? Did I judge myself in the light of my own mother's natural capabilities? She was seriously a rockstar in the mothering department. And then there are those abortions—both Mom's and my own. Did those impact how I saw myself as a mother?

Does society dictate that motherhood is supposed to be natural? Do we just piggyback on the impossibility of being a woman? Maybe.

Women are supposed to be designed for birthing children. Maybe we are told we should be mothers, and we expect we want to be mothers, but even though I had that *knowing* that was stronger than any other path in my life, it was just not natural for me. But so many of those roles that have felt more natural to me have not given me the same rewards.

Nothing else gives me the same depth of joy as being a mom to my children.

I catch myself now, seeing them in their budding adulthoods, and I am blessed to see them in their adultness. Perhaps their births were not as "natural" as I would have liked, but I still did it. I still had two beautiful babies. I did those nine months of heavy lifting. I raised them into adulthood. My body failed me at breastfeeding. Why do I still feel guilty about that one? Now that they are in their twenties, I really need to let go of that burden.

The guilt of divorce? It's time to let that one go, too. We had to make that choice for all of us to be better humans. The eclectic choices we have made are far from that white-picket-fence version of marriage and the life I once believed in. My children have two dads. I have had not one, but two marriages. One gave me our amazing children. The second gave me partnership and true love, and it continues to teach me how to love myself more. I am grateful that both my current and ex-husbands tolerate one another. They both have places on my yearly holiday card.

My mom made her choices. I had to make my own, too. We both struggled with ambivalence about our own decisions. I wish she was here and I could talk to her about this, but I am certain in some alternate universe, we have had this conversation and she knows.

And at the end of the day, I wouldn't have it any other way. It is still really hard to be a mom. The role is still hard for me. But, maybe it is time to show myself a little grace and give myself a little credit. Maybe I am not a bad mom at all, just honestly acknowledge my limitations and accept them. And forgiving myself.

Maybe the hardest role really isn't the hardest; it's just the most complicated.

I am a *good* mom.

About the Author

Best-selling author, speaker, and educator Jessica Goldmuntz Stokes is an entrepreneur at heart. Always seeking her own growth and truth, she teaches and performs belly dance and practices therapeutic touch and Reiki. She is a daughter, a mom, a wife, a friend, and a caregiver. She has navigated multiple family members with Alzheimer's, dementia, and Parkinson's. She is an avid labyrinth-walker, a trained Veriditas Labyrinth facilitator, and a published author of *Seeking Clarity in the Labyrinth, A Daughter's Journey Through Alzheimer's*. She also contributed to the anthology *Planting the Seed: Lessons to Cultivate a Brighter Future*. She provides Labyrinth workshops, lectures, and retreats for anyone experiencing change, loss, or growth.

linktr.ee/jagstokes

Chapter 5

...AND...

BY BRANDEE MELCHER

"They did the best they could... and they did harm." Jeni interjected.

I stared at the screen, partially annoyed at the interjection and completely dumbfounded by what Jeni said. It was my monthly shamanic-drumming therapy session, and this was the first time I felt my brain break. I had been seeing Jeni Dahn for several months now and didn't realize we were just now getting into the depths.

"What? What did you say?" I couldn't process what Jeni had just said.

*"They did the best they could **and** they did harm. The way you say* 'they did the best they could,' *you're excusing their behavior. Excusing their behavior ignores your pain. Both things are true."*

"I'm not excusing them." I immediately said. A rehearsed answer that had been said so many times it was a reflex, and yet this time...I felt the weight of my response. My body felt jittery as my eyes looked to focus on something else in my bedroom other than the screen so Jeni couldn't see the tears beginning to form.

Aware that I had stumbled upon a potential mental landmine, Jeni gently continued. *"Yes, you are. Each time you say, '*They did the best they could,' *you completely ignore your pain and hurt that you've experienced over the years. You're ignoring yourself. You're ignoring little Brandee and all she went through. You're not allowing yourself to begin healing. Little Brandee has carried a lot of the pain with nowhere for it to go because it's been excused for others' comfort."*

Everything Jeni said made sense and was true. I always spoke of my childhood lightly, skipping over parts and quickly following up with a joke so people wouldn't feel uncomfortable with what was just shared—so **they** wouldn't feel bad.

Panic began to set in as the tears trickled down my flushed cheeks. I hate crying and I was doing everything I could to silence the wail that I felt bubbling up inside. Something had been released in these past five minutes that I didn't know how to stop. The tidal wave of buried pain, resentment, and anger was coming up and Jeni knew I needed help to manage this.

"Listen to me. Wrap your arms around yourself and call out to little Brandee. Hold her and tell her all the things you'd wanted to hear when you were scared. Let her talk to you and breathe."

I wrapped my arms around my waist as tight as I could. It wasn't right, wasn't tight enough, I was still exposed. I pulled my knees to my chest, wrapped arms around my knees, squeezed and rocked while Jeni drummed and the tears burned my face and soaked the knees of my sweatpants.

*They did the best they could **and** they did harm and I'm so sorry. You've been hurting for a long time. We've been hurting for a long time. I'm going to do my best to protect both of us—it's up to me now. We won't ever be in those positions again. I promise. I love you.*

Jeni's drumming maintained a calm sound, like a heartbeat, as little Brandee and I sat together for the first time acknowledging our lifetime of pain. Me finally understanding why I could never accept my parents' apologies and why there will always be a ravine between us. Little Brandee *finally* feeling seen and being able to breathe.

～

For the longest time, I did not see or want motherhood in my future. Growing up in the environment that I did, I saw little reason to bring another human into this world. Existence was hard enough. There was a constant struggle for money, attention, and safety. Marriage and children seemed to be the cause of most of my parents' problems. They set the example for what I didn't want in life without ever giving much of a guide for what I would want in life. So, I moved away from what I knew I didn't want: being a parent at 17 or 20 (the ages of my parents when I was born) and focused instead on checking the *"right"* societal boxes.

- HIGH-SCHOOL DIPLOMA ✓
- COLLEGE DEGREE ✓
- SALARIED JOB ✓
- HOUSE ✓
- MASTER'S DEGREE ✓
- MARRIED LIFE WITHOUT CHILDREN ✓

There was a brief moment, maybe a month, somewhere in between checking the boxes that there may have been something growing. The smell of stale cigarettes sent me rushing to the bathroom and I found myself kneeling over the toilet. As I worked to calm the nausea, the very real realization that I could be pregnant began to sink in. We were not trying to get pregnant and yet here I was. Admittedly I didn't always take my pill on time; there were days where I'd take two at a time, so the possibility of being pregnant was very real. It was much too early to take a pregnancy test and I told my then-husband to keep him aware of the potential life change coming. He was scared, nervous, and happy. I was unsure. I didn't want to be pregnant yet and I began to envision the future.

It wasn't all doom and gloom. It was going to be better than I had growing up. It was going to be happier. I could do this. We could do this. I was calmer about the potential, even if it wasn't happening when I wanted it.

Then my cycle came—much heavier than usual and only a day or two late. I was very relieved and yet...we started to have a serious conversation about being pregnant sooner than originally planned. It seemed like a good plan—not great, but good and doable. All the reasons we had to start sooner, though, were for everyone else— everyone but me.

Thankfully I have one of the best cousins anyone could ask for, and she reminded me that being pregnant was about me. *What did I want?* Sure, I could handle a baby, but did I really want one now? Just because I *may* have been pregnant, doesn't mean I needed to change my timeline because I wasn't pregnant now. So, we waited and on my 30th birthday we heard the heartbeat of our oldest daughter for the first time.

The path to pregnancy wasn't as easy as I had thought it would be. I had heard so many stories about people becoming pregnant immediately after stopping birth control that I was sure that was going to be our story. Afterall, there was the very real possibility I was pregnant a year or so before when I wasn't trying, so why not now?

Pregnancy didn't come as quickly as we had hoped. I was miserable being off of birth control. I was tired of the tests, dyes, and counts. I knew I wasn't open to IVF treatments, so if this didn't happen naturally, it wasn't going to happen. I began to mentally make peace with the fact that I wouldn't get pregnant and we would turn towards adoption. I was desperate to get back on birth control, accepting the fact I had failed at this. That we had failed at the most basic thing humans—all animals—are supposed to do.

I was conflicted.

I really didn't know if I wanted to be pregnant and yet I was disappointed that it wasn't happening after months of trying. I didn't know if I really wanted to change the life we currently had, and yet I was ready for the next thing, which seemed like parenthood.

And then there she was. A positive pregnancy test when I was ready to call my doctor to renew my birth-control prescription. I felt relief, excitement, and fear. I thought, "Here's what we had been trying for and now I don't know what to do now that's it's here."

I approached pregnancy with pragmatism. I knew at any moment this could be over. While I accepted and knew I was growing a baby, I also knew I didn't *have* a baby until he or she was safely on the other side nine months later. I was afraid to get too emotionally attached to something that might not make it all the way. I had no logical reasoning for this, as I had never had a miscarriage, but l still maintained an emotional distance from my growing baby.

I was also wanting to hold on to the Brandee I was becoming, thinking that if pregnancy couldn't change me, then neither would motherhood. However, I was in denial. Pregnancy had changed me. I was more conscientious when I drove...more mindful about my food choices...silently making plans for life after birth. Evaluating clothing on its longevity past pregnancy into postpartum and breastfeeding. I was attempting to maintain my individuality while slowly making daily changes for the next person to enter my life.

Then on the car ride home from the hospital, I considered giving up my dream of climbing the corporate ladder to become CEO. I more than considered it; it became a topic of conversation and a loose plan was formed. We agreed that I would return to work after my six weeks of maternity leave and then the next year would be spent working towards becoming a single-corporate-income household while I figured out some way to be able to work from home. Unfortunately, the plan never became reality because no one told us newborn land is about straight survival. There was little room for additional mental expansion outside of figuring out how to keep a tiny human and yourself alive. Then, just as there was a bit of light at the end of the tunnel, we found ourselves pregnant with our surprise second shortly after celebrating our oldest's first birthday. I knew my second daughter was there the moment she was conceived and attempted to talk myself out of the pregnancy due to the difficulty experienced in the first. However, seeing that second pregnancy test put a smile on my face and I approached this pregnancy slightly less pragmatically than the first. I had a sense of security and I often reminded myself to stay grounded; I wanted her to be here before I fully celebrated and accepted the life to be.

Soon we had two little girls barely under two, and I found myself uninspired by the life we had. I wanted more. I needed more.

I loved our daughters dearly and yet, I needed to find the old Brandee. What I didn't realize is the Brandee that existed before motherhood was gone. She was still alive in my memories, but she was never coming back. I was a new Brandee, and I had no idea how to be this person. I had spent thirty years building my previous self and was too busy with my new life to recognize when she left.

I was existing. I was in a space where I had barely gotten to know my previous self, didn't know who I was at this moment, and wasn't sure how to move forward. I enjoyed motherhood and yet I kept waiting, wanting, desiring my old life to return. I had had two major life events occur twenty-one months apart from each other, and I expected that I would stay the same. All of the mothers before and around me seemed to enjoy motherhood. They never spoke of life prior to motherhood. It seemed they forgot who they were before, or it didn't matter. Meanwhile, I felt like I was having an identity crisis.

I finally found my people. My life coach at the time mentioned Sara Dean, host of the podcast *The Shameless Mom Academy,* and I was hooked.

Here were other highly motivated mothers who also wanted to be their own person. Here were other women who acknowledged the multitudes that existed in each of us. We were having real conversations about our lives. We were in the mess together. We were allowed to talk about all the chaos that it is to be a mother and a woman and a wife and a driven professional and a friend and an individual.

I didn't feel like an outsider to this motherhood thing anymore. I was a full human experiencing a full range of emotions as I grappled with what it meant to care for two tiny humans as I worked to heal myself.

~

In the process of healing myself, I came to realize my marriage was not the marriage I wanted. I wanted better. I wanted a marriage where I was chosen. I decided to end my marriage after eleven years because my husband chose alcohol over me. Over us.

I made one of the hardest and best decisions of my life, of our lives. **And I did harm.**

I changed all our lives because I wanted a better life for all of us—especially me and my daughters. I didn't want my daughters growing up with a resentful or angry mother. Had I stayed married, it would have meant everyone would have been happy while I slowly died. That was not a trade-off I was willing to make, nor an example I was willing to live.

Knowing I've caused hurt to my daughters is a weight I carry every day. And knowing they will have a better life ahead of them helps make that weight a little lighter.

(The rest of my story can be read in *The Break: Rediscovering Our Inner Knowing.*)

~

Motherhood has been a continual practice of allowing and accepting multiple truths to exist in the same moment.

Wanting to hold your baby tight the entire day and wishing that no one would touch you for the next week. Feeling your heart melt as they say *"Momma"* and being annoyed that they can't figure something out without you. Desiring for life to return to pre-motherhood existence and knowing you could never go back to life before you held their tiny body in your arms.

Motherhood is a healing and, at times, traumatizing existence. I've become a better person because I've made a conscious decision to be better. At first, I was healing for them. I didn't want to parent them the way I had been parented.

I wanted to love them for the life we were making, not resent them for the life I had given up.

I never wanted them to feel like a burden, like an obligation. They were a conscious choice we had made, I had made, and love was the most important legacy I could give them. And I could only give this to them by acknowledging, beginning to accept, and healing the multitudes within myself. Motherhood is the path I unknowingly needed to take to begin my healing journey.

There are moments that touch the core of my soul and I'm brought to tears. There are moments that are deeply triggering and remind me to keep healing. There are moments of soul exhaustion and I'm reminded to pause and rest. Motherhood has been, and will continue to be, deeply rewarding...even when there are days I want to quit.

About the Author

Brandee Melcher is a woman, author, and mother who is continually working to undo the lessons she was taught growing up that no longer serve her or her children. She is teaching her daughters and other women in her circle to pay attention to their inner knowing by taking the time to focus inward and quiet the outside world with tips found in her weekly newsletter.

Brandee lives just outside of Raleigh, North Carolina in her house that is in a constant state of improvement—much like herself. In between raising her two daughters and the corporate job, she spends most of her time reading, working in her garden, going for jogs, and visiting lighthouses in all shapes and sizes.

linktr.ee/brandeemelcher807

Chapter 6

(GREATLY) MODIFIED PARENTING GOALS
BY JENNIFER RHODE

When I was living in New York in my twenties spending Sundays enjoying boozy brunches after taking an early yoga class and wandering through the Chelsea flea market—which is sadly now all condominiums—clutching a giant coffee from the bodega on my corner, I had all kinds of ideas about what my life would be like when I had children. I would, of course, still live in the city, but I would have a huge loft, rather than my run-down Holly Hobbie-sized apartment and my children would just slip into my life without disrupting my routines. They would come to brunch with me wearing adorable outfits and contribute witty, charming stories to the conversation, enchanting the waiter so much that we were sent a plate of free beignets each week. They would use their cutlery properly and keep their napkins in their laps and they would *not* whine or cry at the table like all the other bratty, poorly parented children in the world. They would be like this because I was going to be a *good* mother who paid attention and set boundaries and generally just had my stuff together.

Now, after more than seventeen years of parenting, I have been truly humbled by the task of taking care of other people. And my standards of success have been mightily adjusted. I *have* been that mother whose child was wailing and begging for Cheetos in the checkout line. I *have* been the mother whose child had unbrushed hair and a crusty face and was still wearing pajamas to the diner (*not* Tartine, the adorable corner bistro, in the West Village) for breakfast (*not* brunch—no child can wait until nearly noon to eat their first meal of the day). I *have* been the mother whose child rolls their eyes and shoots out snark and sassafras and forgets to say, "please" and "thank you." And I *have* been the mother who completely loses it and yells at her kids and bursts into tears with frustration and fury that the people I *grew* in my body (and painfully pushed *out* of it, which I poignantly remember even though everyone says you forget how much it hurts as soon as it is over) could be so rude and thoughtless.

So now I try to celebrate the small victories. In the fall of my daughter's fourth-grade year, we had a lot of barfing at my house. The school nurse called and said I had to pick Lucy up early from school one afternoon. As soon as we got home, she threw up about a million times. And *all* of it went into the toilet or the bowl I stationed next to her on the sofa. I honestly could not have been prouder. Some parents get really excited about a perfect test score, a hat trick in their kid's soccer game or when their child makes something cool for the science fair. And those things *do* make me happy, but the fact that my daughter could be that sick and I didn't have to scrub vomit off my sofa, the rug or even her clothes made my heart swell to bursting. And I think she set a good example because a few days later, Hank, our dog, came down with kennel cough. He had interviewed for doggie daycare and must have picked it up while on the test playdate. He started coughing so violently (poor baby) that he was also spitting up. He could not reach the toilet (his legs are only about seven inches long) but he *did* take care to only throw up on the easy-to-mop wood floor. When he'd start hacking, he'd leap off the sofa or the bed and make sure that his regurgitation was not near anything difficult to clean. Again, I was filled with immense love, pride and gratitude.

I am not good with messiness, especially if it is bloody or smelly and comes out of your body. I had a very hard time getting through the period when my children's teeth were falling out and they were left with bright red gaps in their mouths that they kept making me look at because they were so excited. I would be the worst doctor. Most of the time when I am watching *Grey's Anatomy,* I have my eyes covered and just listen to the dialogue so I don't have to be subjected to the gruesome wounds and unexpected vomit, guts, urine or feces that show up regularly in the ER. I do push myself to power through the show each week (for decades now) because that is where I get all my medical knowledge, but it is not easy.

And frankly, I don't think anyone should have to be exposed to such grossness if they are not getting paid (which mothers never are... at least for that!) So if I can raise children (and a puppy) who are considerate enough to minimize damage when they have the stomach flu or are brushing their teeth (who appreciates being left with toothpaste spit shellacked onto the sink bowl?) or going number two (definitely *no one* likes being confronted with poop cement!) then I will consider it a job well done. My kids may not go to the Olympics, get into Harvard, win a Pulitzer or even tell the most engaging story at brunch, but I am making it my mission that by the time they leave my house, they know how to take care of their own bodily debris. It is really a metaphor for being a generally good citizen, and I am sure that their future housemates and girlfriends and spouses will appreciate my good work and dedication.

UPDATE: A mother's work is never done. I found these texts written by my nine-year-old daughter on my phone (she didn't yet have one) to her older brother when he was sitting right next to her on the sofa (wrestling for the corner spot) watching a show...double screening! Absolutely tip-top parenting.

Lucy to Theo:

I don't know *where* she picked up that language (or that spelling), but clearly, I can't rest on my parenting laurels just because she vomited perfectly into the toilet.

About the Author

Jennifer Rhode is an interior designer, writer and mother out of Boulder, Colorado. She works on both residential and commercial projects and is known for her modern, minimal, yet warm aesthetic. She previously worked as a fashion stylist in New York City and San Francisco before launching her design firm in Boulder. She writes interior stories for local magazines as well as her lifestyle blog: www.jenniferrhode.com/blog. Jennifer delights in her two spunky children and her adorable dog, Hank.

linktr.ee/jenniferrhode

Chapter 7

RELATIONSHIP REVIVAL
BY REAH HAGUES

<u>Summary</u>

The year was 1999 and I was fourteen years old. I met a grown-@$$ man on a chat site I was way too young to be on, and within the next year became a teenage single parent with a mountain of struggles, triumphs, tests, growth, pain, and recovery ahead. I started my journey as a mother being emotionally unintelligent, which was reflected in all of my relationships. This chapter will explain how you can, and why you should, turn your struggles into triumphs by learning healthy relationship navigation through emotional intelligence.

EMOTIONALLY UNINTELLIGENT

How did I become a stable, prosperous, emotionally intelligent entrepreneur with healthy relationships? I acknowledged my unhealthy relationships and educated myself to achieve the goals I finally realized I needed to have. We have to allow ourselves time to heal, grow, and evolve. How can you cater to your needs as a mother and positively influence your healing journey? By working to improve communication with those around you by responding to hard times and difficult people with healthy communication.

Most of my unhealthy relationships began very early in my life. My parents divorced when I was little, and my mother and I relocated to North Carolina from South Carolina, where I grew up. This move created distance between my father and me, but being closer to her family afforded my mother more help and allowed her to raise me in a healthier environment. My grandmother helped my mother with me, and naturally, due to differences in child rearing and the stress of having a child in the home of an empty nester, my grandmother and I had a problematic relationship. I went from living with my father and mother to seeing my father every other weekend, which was naturally traumatic. I adored my father, and of my few childhood memories, the majority are reflected in pictures of him and me.

Unhealthy relationships impacted my life, and my unhealthy relationships affected all areas of my life. I began unhealthy relationships with men because after being raped, I figured it was better to control the situation by being promiscuous and expecting men only to want sex rather than be taken advantage of unexpectedly. My relationships with men had been deeply affected by both sexual assault and my relationship with my own father (which I desperately denied for decades). By the time I was twenty-three, I had already given birth to four children—two as a single teen and two with my then husband. I started to distance myself from my father more due to family racism and a dislike for his alcoholism and the actions associated with it. I, too, would later have an unhealthy relationship with alcohol, which led to a few worse decisions.

Not having both parents in the home generally leads to not knowing what it looks like to provide a healthy relationship for your own children. I was not a healthy parent and did not exemplify healthy relationships with my children when I was younger. It may have been my age, life experience, lack of knowledge, or a combination of the three. Being a child of divorce does not mean you will naturally parent your children in an unhealthy manner. It does mean it will likely be difficult if you do not educate yourself on healthy relationships or have a positive example of such in an older couple, such as an aunt/uncle, cousins, siblings, or community members in healthy relationships. I did not have this perception until later in life because, like most people, I thought it would be fine—the kids would get older and do better. My thought was that I was already an adult, and my issues were from trauma I could not change. I do not regret all of my parenting, as my children are responsible, sensible, respectful young adults. However, I did engage in some aggressive parenting, that came from being angry; I expressed that through my parenting (in more ways than simply being a strict parent). I acted out of emotion in response to stress instead of choosing more productive behaviors at the moment. Now, I have a lot more conversations and implement better communication. It is still a consistent work in progress. But, I now know that yelling, not practicing healthy communication, and not practicing conversation preparation (preparing a response instead of just reacting) are all unhealthy ways to parent.

At fourteen, I met a man on an adult chatline as I pretended to be older, and he pretended to be younger. We met up quickly and, after a while, began what I deemed to be my first consensual sexual relationship. Upon ending that relationship, I began smoking marijuana a lot and going out with different men while my mother watched my toddler. My behavior strained my relationship with my mother as my focus was much more on men than on school or anything she tried to teach me about life or motherhood. Society automatically predicts teenage parents to fail in most aspects of their life. In my almost twenty-four years of parenting, I wish I had known earlier in life how much of a positive impact healthy communication could have on many of my relationships. Healthy communication skills and emotional intelligence have taught me as a mother that I can face my fears, power through my struggles, improve my overall wellness, and raise better humans by simply becoming educated and making time for my parental health improvement. From a child raising children to a successful mother, wife, author, business owner, and communicator, I got to where I am by nurturing the child inside myself, and learning how to provide patience to my children while applying it to the adult in me.

INTERNAL GROWTH

I took time away from relationships that were harmful to me, I allowed other people time to grow, and I accepted myself for who I am instead of who I was. After receiving two DUIs in two years, I decided it was time to get my life in order by kicking the alcohol addiction I was cursed with genetically and environmentally. I also chose to stop smoking to better my children's health and my own. In 2015, I started writing my autobiography, and it was such an emotional experience that I put it away for a few years before picking it back up to turn it into an actual published book. Throughout the writing experience, I started to allow myself to feel emotions I had locked away for so long. I spent so much time being excellent at expressing anger and horrible at expressing healthy emotions that learning to do so felt overwhelming. While writing chapters like "Daddy Issues" (about my relationship with my father as well as the fathers of my children), "Mommy Issues" (mostly about my evolution as a mother), and "Traumas & Health," I took small breaks to collect myself and work through emotions. These chapters took me back to times when I had difficulty making good choices and allowed me to reflect on the growth process of healing from those choices and their consequences.

We will never successfully respond if all we do is react. Once I started working with mentors I obtained through podcasting and writing, I started learning so many things I would never have thought to utilize to build healthy relationships. Communication is vital, as cliché as it sounds, and once I learned to focus on communication, so many of my relationship dynamics changed. For example, others do not know what we think if we do not vocalize it. As much as we would love for our spouse to "know how we feel," it is absurd to expect them to do so. I had to learn that I could not expect things from my husband that I did not verbalize to him. Communication is not the only key in romantic relationships. My relationship with my stepmother started to heal when I realized I could not blame her for my father's choices as much as I wanted to blame her for his actions. I also began to understand by having conversations with her that she only wanted the best for me, and what I deemed controlling was just simple boundary implementation. I went my whole life thinking she was trying to control me because she hated my mother. In reality, she was the one who always drove me home when I threw a fit, wanting to go home because they put rules in place. In hindsight, had I followed the rules they had in place, I never would have gotten pregnant as a teen or gotten into smoking marijuana. My perspective changed after I conversed with her rather than continuing to assume the worst.

I started mending strained and broken relationships once I began to learn more about mental health, including regulating my emotions; I learned that I could determine the trajectory of my relationships on my own! In 2020, I returned to school to obtain my master's degree in psychology. This journey was fun because it also included my five-year-old starting kindergarten online. We would sit side-by-side for the thirty minutes they kept kids on for class—yes, an entire thirty minutes. I was in shock the first week as I thought school time for him would also be schoolwork time for me, thanks to COVID-19-induced e-learning! Frustrating start aside, the education I obtained by earning my psychology degree taught me healthy communication and listening skills, and most of all, why these are important and how they affect our relationships. Once I began my journey through education in psychology, it was like a lightning bolt hit me; my life choices were both a result of my trauma and my lack of emotional intelligence. I also had to learn that I could not blame everyone else for how I reacted to my trauma as an adult. Changing habits, especially lifestyles, can be challenging but is always worth the hard work.

LONG-TERM SUCCESS

How can you obtain and maintain healthy, successful relationships with others and yourself? First, start with understanding your trauma and how it impacts your relationships. We experience things that impact who we are in the world. Controlling my feelings about being raped by being promiscuous sounded ridiculous until I obtained an education in psychology about trauma, how it affects our brain, and how we respond to stressors. We have to understand that we cannot do better if we do not know better. I grew up around cigarette smokers, alcohol abuse, unhealthy emotional regulation, unhealthy communication, and poverty. Naturally, since I became a mother so young, I practiced life in the manner I knew how. I smoked cigarettes, I had unhealthy relationships, I drank more often than I should have to deal with my pain, and I was aggressive in raising my kids because I thought aggression was strictness. Like myself, many people do not know where to begin because they have not been shown examples of healthy relationships.

Second, learn about and practice accountability. I was a "do as I say, not as I do" parent in the past. Why would any child do what an adult says when the adult doesn't do it themselves? I did not want my kids to start smoking, and I needed to be healthier for them, so I quit smoking. It took about a year off and on, but one day, I decided my children were more important, so I quit. I did not want the pattern to continue like I had seen in other family members. It was the same with teen pregnancy: I refused to let that "generational blip" continue in my family, so I began to educate my children on sex and STDs before they reached puberty. I also taught them about their bodies, what to expect, etc., because I want to educate them about life as much as possible. I know I cannot prevent or change everything in life, but I can prepare them as much as possible. I also dive deep into research when I want to learn something new, and I love to share it with everyone around me. I am not saying everyone has to go to college; finding healthy practices can be as simple as watching YouTube videos or doing research online.

Third, implement healthy communication in all your relationships. Most often in relationships, we focus on what the other person has done. Even after what they have done, we struggle with responding to it rather than reacting to it at the moment, creating a lot of emotional tension and unresolved anger. Relationships—

whether romantic, familial, parent-child, or professional—are work. Understanding how healthy relationships function is imperative. Understanding our trauma and how to take accountability for our actions gives us the knowledge to be accountable for how we communicate with others. Trauma does not go away, but how we react to it decreases the power we allow our trauma to have over us. Healthy communication is the key to delivering the correct message. For example, if a conversation turns into an argument, you can take a second to evaluate and reflect on how you can control your wording to get your point across in a positive, calm, and productive manner. Healthy and effective communication can be achieved by maintaining eye contact (not communicating while doing something else like looking at your phone, etc.) and communicating in person rather than writing whenever possible so the communication receiver can see facial cues and body language, and hear tone to avoid unintentional negative inferences.

Our accomplishments can positively impact our relationships. How can my accomplishments help readers? I frequently focus on emotional intelligence, healthy communication, and vulnerability in my coaching business. I also put this into play in my podcast. Last year, I had my eldest son's father on in a series of three episodes called "Getting to Know Fred." This interview was not easy as we have an unhealthy history of communication. Implementing my learned skills allowed me to converse with a man I was angry at for many years. On my podcast, *Just the WHO of Us,* I bring guests on to discuss their areas of expertise, life experiences, and accomplishments. With an eye toward relationship improvement, my first guest on *Just the WHO of Us* was my ex-husband. We fought and yelled for years before we had another civil conversation, and about four years later, I took his idea to start a podcast and made it a reality! He is no longer a co-host, but that is due to scheduling rather than a relationship conflict, as he has been a recurring guest! My new podcast, *Mom Brain with Falolity*, features my co-host and I talking to women in parental or caregiver roles about motherhood. My workbooks work side-by-side with the *Mom Brain* podcast and family and relationship coaching to lead clients from the beginning of child-rearing through personal growth and development, teaching them how to be the best parents they can be regardless of who they are and what they've been through. The podcast allows me to showcase my skills in communicating with other mothers about the many aspects of their parenting journey. I try to teach that healthy communication is critical; love yourself and all the unhealed parts of you that deserve patience!

Often, we communicate in a hostile, unhealthy manner in reaction to our surroundings or past. Reacting to the feeling of being provoked, disagreed with, argued with, etc. (which children naturally do, especially when they are at the age where they know more and are more emotionally driven to debate or defend their intelligence) usually causes an emotionally charged response. While we feel validated (and at times, we are), nothing productive comes from emotionally charged reactions. Effective communication results in a calmer, more well-thought-out reaction informed by rational, patient, and clearer thoughts. Most of the time, this produces solutions rather than attacks or reactive and unproductive words. How can you change your relationships by evolving your communication skills and improving your emotional intelligence today?

About the Author

Reah Hagues holds degrees in psychology, holistic mental health and wellness, and Christian studies. Throughout her life, she has blossomed from a teenage single mother in poverty to a successful entrepreneur. Changing relationship perspectives motivates all she does. She guides others through relationship trauma with the result of improved perspective and repaired relationships. In this way, she is building a world where everyone can be safe, successful, and healthy through faith, love, and equality! Residing in beautiful North Carolina, she is also the author of parenting workbooks and an autobiography. She is the mother of five children and a wife to the most amazing man she has ever met. She loves her family with all her heart, and they are the reason for everything she does.

linktr.ee/reahhagues

Chapter 8

MISSING CHILDREN
BY SANDI PHINNEY

How can I need so badly to escape my children, and yet miss them so fiercely at the same time? It is the forever question, always present, never answerable, simply one of the many realities of motherhood. There is no harm in the dichotomy unless you let it eat away at your confidence and sense of self, eroding your ability to appreciate the joy of a moment, with or without them. You might do that first, as I did; there is no shame in it. For me, the lesson was a long journey, and the tipping point came during a gale in the Gulf of Alaska. Being thousands of miles away from them while Mother Nature was trying to kill me taught me to miss my kids. Purely, and without guilt. And with it, a gratefulness that my kids were not with me, not because of the danger of weather and ravishing waves, but because there was something that I had to do for myself.

It wasn't that I hadn't missed them before. I had been away from them for workdays, mom nights out, even the occasional overnight conference. I would talk with them on the phone, their high-pitched voices regaling me with their daily adventures sparking a familiar lump in my throat. But the missing was always tinged with guilt that I had needed to escape them—whether for work or sanity—and, even worse, guilt that I enjoyed that time away.

In so many moments of maternal desperation, I *had* wanted to flee from my kids. From their clinging, sucking, crying, whining, running, revving, constant noise. I didn't know it was normal to need that escape. I felt something was wrong with me, that I didn't have the maternal skills to handle it all. And yet, twenty minutes after I was away from them, the missing of them would appear in goosebumps and stomach knots long before my mind caught up. On the first day I went back to work, I left my crying baby in a stranger's arms. My belly tightened, and my breasts tingled and swelled heavily with milk as I tried to take notes in a meeting. I hoped the warm liquid wouldn't show through my sweater as I felt it spilling into my padded bra. My brain and body felt the missing deep down, even though I knew it would only be a few short hours before I could hold my baby in my arms again and let my milk and breath release. And all the while, I felt joy in being back at work, even for a few hours. Adults to talk with. Problems other than diaper leakage to solve. I relished those moments of work time, which only made the guilt of leaving my child in another's arms that much more potent. Did the fact that I enjoyed and craved being back in the office this much mean I wasn't meant to have children?

It wasn't just work I wanted to escape to; it was also dream worlds. Quiet ones. During all those early mornings—how many were there? —I remember lying on the bed putting on a training video (the longest one I could find) for Andy so he could watch it while I tried to grab a few more minutes of sleep. I fantasized about being in a room in a castle on a soft feather bed piled up with blankets, a fireplace to keep me warm, thick stone walls to keep out the noise, and staff to care for the kids when they woke up at 5:00 in the morning. I transported myself to that world over and over, imagining the quiet walls, the feather bed pulling me in, the luxury of closing my eyes and going back to sleep. And then I felt the guilt surge, seeping in like poison to all those folds of my brain. How selfish was I that I would put a screen in front of my 18-month-old baby so that I could sleep more? I felt that overwhelming, never-ending, bone-dissolving fatigue will lead you to do anything you can to catch an extra moment of sleep. And then we'd finally get up, I'd have my coffee, and he'd sit on my lap while I read to him. I'd be so full of love, and love that came out in the words I read to him, as they still do and always will. And for a while, I didn't want to escape. The irony is that in the castle of that dream world, even though I slept alone on a soft feather bed, my kids were still with me there. I took them with me but carved out a room for myself where I could rest and do what I needed to do to recover strength.

When they became toddlers, it was the incessant noise I couldn't handle. I needed an escape from the clatter and clanging. More than once, I went outside and sat in my car, the only quiet place I could think of, and the silence flooded through me. My shoulders dropped; my jaw released. As I closed my eyes, I could feel the flood of calm and quiet wash over me like when you pull yourself under the water of a warm, deep bath. And then the physical missing would kick in, a guilt that showed up in my stomach, then my heart, then my mind. You know those moments—when you have to leave the room because you're crying; and you close your eyes and let time stop; and you imagine that wave of silence enclosing you, engulfing your veins, brain, body, and heart. And then you get up and go back because that's what moms do.

I wondered where the guilt came from. Was it from my grandmother, who disapproved of working mothers? Was it from my own sense of inadequacy that I couldn't be everything to my kids? Maybe it was an innate, maternal, animalistic instinct—something that kept us from walking away and never turning back. Because how many mothers have not had that fantasy of just walking away into another life?

All these moments away were temporary—a few hours here, a few days there. A constant pull of fleeing and missing and guilting. But out on that sailboat in the middle of the Gulf of Alaska gale, something changed. I was being ravaged by wind and waves and icy rain, and the kids were playing contentedly on solid, dry, warm, sunny earth with doting grandparents. We had been sailing the Pacific when Covid-19 hit, and it had already separated us for months.

My husband, Tom, had ended up in French Polynesia while I was stuck in Mexico with the kids. When we finally reunited in Hawaii months later and decided to sail home via Alaska, I had wanted them with us. I didn't want to separate the family again. But Tom had said, "No. I want you to learn what you're capable of, and that's not going to happen with the kids aboard." I assented and flew them home to my parents so they could play safely on dry land for a month while we delivered our battered selves and boat across the North Pacific.

Out on that boat, two and a half weeks into our north-Pacific passage, with the salt wind pushing us hard through those bitter, biting waves, I missed the kids viscerally. My chest warmed with the feeling of their heat against me as if they were sitting in my lap in the middle of that icy, watery wilderness. Andy felt so real against me, I could literally feel his hips and bony butt digging into my thighs. If I closed my eyes, I felt him leaning back against me, his little heart racing. He grabbed my arm and pulled it around him. I could sense his older brother, Dylan, snuggling up under my other arm, not to be outdone. I could smell his platinum hair and hear his engine noises as he rolled his Hot Wheel over my leg. Everyone wanted a piece of mom, a piece of lap, of skin, of attention. If I kept my eyes closed, they were there with me. If I kept my eyes closed, I didn't see the twelve-foot waves outside. I didn't see the walls of water or the endless gray horizon of the North Pacific. There was nothing here. There were no islands, no people. The last bird had left us long ago. No whales had appeared to guide us—whales that would have captivated Andy, who taught himself to read from a reference book about whales, dolphins, and porpoises. No, there were no animals, no visible life. No vital life.

Only occasional pieces of trash; a depressed husband; a nostalgic wife; and a seasick, elderly cat. The waves battered the boat from all sides. The wind ripped through the rigging, howling and screeching. Metal clanged, and fiberglass flexed. I closed my eyes and felt the icy rain and sea spray pelt my cheeks. It was good they weren't here. Despite my deep-down, desperate missing, it was good they weren't here. I was so sick myself, I could barely stand my watch, and it was all I could do to dress and face the weather. I could not have taken care of them. Worry would have stolen my energy and driven my fear if they had been here. And that was when the missing became purer and began to lose the stain of guilt.

"I have not escaped or abandoned them," I told myself. As hard as it was to separate the family again, there was something I had to do. I had to learn what I was capable of. For my family, for the boat, for our sailing trip, yes. But mostly for myself. That was the difference. I needed time to do something for myself, to be out there honing and using my skills without distraction. It didn't feel selfish; it felt like the safer answer. It wasn't a revelation or something that sunk in immediately. It took time. I knew logically that it was the right thing to do, but the feeling that we *could have, should have, might have* stayed together stuck with me for a while. I had to repeat over and over to myself: It was the right decision. I need to learn what I am capable of.

Now, years later, as they are older and easier, and the memories of the desperation begin to fade, I begin to wonder about that need to escape—and why I felt so guilty about it. What was it that pulled, pushed, and urged me to want to escape so intensely? As I dive deeper into the why, I can see now that it wasn't really to get away from the noise and the tugging (though that was part of it because there is only so much sensory stimulation a body can take). It was because I needed to remember who *I* was *without* all the noise and tugging. I was losing myself and no longer was in touch with who I had been before. I needed to escape because I needed the time and peace to turn inward, to hear the voice of my heart and mind instead of the clatter of pots and pans and baby cries. If I had realized that at the time, perhaps I would have felt a lot less guilty about the constant need to escape and then having the missing tinged with the guilt that I should be there with them and not serving my own needs. I am now at peace with missing my children, a hard-fought battle.

Missing them doesn't have to mean I have done something wrong in being away from them. And wanting to escape from them does not mean that I don't love them. I am a better parent because of the missing. It makes me realize how much I love them and encourages me to value more the time that I have with them.

My love for them is not diminished by the need to be alone. In fact, my time alone serves to create the identity I need to love them more. To show them that I have a life and passions that are my own and that bring me joy—writing and reading, skiing and swimming, travel and long discussions with friends over wine or tea. The more I lose myself, the more I resent motherhood. The more I am allowed to be me, the more I can proudly wear motherhood as a *part* of my identity, but not all of it. And if they learn it and see it, maybe they will model it for their own kids someday. Parenthood is an incredible gift, but so is the passion to pursue your dreams and identity and joys outside of parenthood. And when you do these things, it is okay and normal to miss your kids. And it's also okay *not* to miss them. There is joy in both.

Toward the end of that rough and fatiguing passage to Alaska, when I felt I could do little but stare at the chart and slowly count down each nautical mile, I said to Tom, "It's good they weren't here. They would have had to take care of themselves. It was hard enough just to take care of ourselves."

I no longer felt guilty that we flew them home, that we didn't stay together across the vast North Pacific. At the end of that difficult passage, we arrived in Seward, and I texted my mom to let her know we had arrived.

"The kids are fine," my mom wrote back. "They look forward to seeing you in a few days."

"Thank you," I wrote. "Tell them I miss them."

About the Author

Sandi Phinney is a graduate of Carleton College, the University of Washington, and the University of Massachusetts Boston. She worked as a writing assistant in college and focused much of her international relations studies on German and Slavic literature. She has traveled the world for most of her life for work, study, and her own personal passion, collecting and writing stories along the way. In 2018, her family departed on a two-and-a-half-year sailing adventure around the Pacific, www.sailingkorvessa.com.

Her memoir, *The Crazy: Adventure, Autism, and the Art of Finding Your Way Home*, recounts the parallel odysseys of the ill-fated sailing trip and her own self-discovery. She currently works as the Chief Strategy Officer for Community Action of Skagit County. She lives in Anacortes, Washington with her two kids and a cat.

linktr.ee/SandiPhinney

Chapter 9

THE BETTER SELF FORMULA
BY ERIKA SHALENE HULL

A Compassionate Guide to Self-Preservation

B uckle up, friend, because we're about to dive into the wild ride that is motherhood together. The journey through motherhood is a unique and challenging adventure, filled with overwhelming responsibilities and moments of sheer panic. As mothers and caregivers, we often find ourselves neglecting our well-being while tending to the needs of others. In this chapter, we will explore The BETTER Self Formula – a compassionate and practical guide to building true perseverance that begins with creating the self-preservation needed to navigate the challenges of motherhood and caregiving.

Now, let's get real for a moment. Imagine me, sitting on my couch, legs kicked up – but instead of relaxation, it's pure panic. A broken pelvis, a week-old newborn in one arm, and a three-year-old snuggled on the other side. My five-year-old is sharing kindergarten tales, my ten-year-old is practicing basketball behind me, and my newly-driving 16-year-old is hunting for the car keys. Overwhelmed doesn't even begin to cover it. Being the primary caregiver for FIVE children from the confines of my couch, with the challenge of daily self-care and household responsibilities, hit me hard. Panic set in as my husband returned to work that morning.

And guess what? This wasn't the first rodeo with overwhelming circumstances in my life. But here's the deal – the lessons I've learned from these moments have transformed my ability to navigate over-whelming situations without succumbing to sheer panic. This trans-formation, born from my journey through motherhood, has touched the lives of thousands, especially women and mothers.

My journey started at 20, delivering my first child at 23, and wrap-ping up with the birth of my fifth at 39. Imagine 4.2 years of preg-nancy, 13.1 years of nursing, and a myriad of parenting responsibilities spanning 24 years – that's been my role as the primary parent. Along-side these responsibilities, life threw curveballs: leaving a cult, family estrangement, homelessness, managing diverse careers, dealing with loved ones' addictions, enduring divorce, surviving captivity, and abuse, coping with the tragic loss of my oldest child to suicide, and navigating the complexities of the justice system as a domestic violence survivor. While rebuilding my life, I found safe, secure, and trusting love, navigating through the myriad challenges that accom-pany such a journey.

Now, I'm not here to grab sympathy or ignite comparisons – I'm here to highlight the universal thread of overwhelming experiences embedded in our life journeys. Your path might not mirror mine in-depth, but the shared feelings of overwhelm unite us all. The journey through motherhood, in particular, propels us into a perpetual state of overwhelm, given the inherent challenges of life compounded by the responsibility for another human being's care and survival.

Survival in this journey requires a core foundation of self-preser-vation. Oddly enough, we're seldom taught how to preserve ourselves adequately to navigate the perfectly normal state of overwhelm. The concept of "self-care" is broad and nebulous, with societal expecta-tions loaded with unreasonable demands. It leaves us ill-equipped to handle the multifaceted demands of caregiving, especially in the context of motherhood.

So, how does one survive the whirlwind of motherhood and care-giving without sacrificing personal well-being and identity? The answer lies in cultivating genuine and sustaining self-preservation. And guess what? This need extends beyond caregivers and parents – it's a fundamental requirement for all.

Previous generations were burdened with misguided expectations that failed to serve their well-being. The idea that providing care necessitates self-sacrifice and that motherhood is synonymous with martyrdom has deeply permeated societal norms. The absence of guidance on comprehensive self and life management skills left many navigating life with the vague assurance that they'd figure it out, perpetuating a cycle of mere survival at the cost of personal well-being.

Let's talk about a critical mindset shift – establishing a new norm that prioritizes self-preservation to ensure individuals **can** care for others adequately. Contrary to societal beliefs, putting oneself first is not selfish; it's a prerequisite for effective caregiving. Because really, how can you fulfill caregiving responsibilities without first tending to your well-being?

For many, ingrained beliefs in prioritizing others over oneself, coupled with unrealistic expectations and misconceptions about self-care, create an environment where self-preservation is an afterthought. In times of extreme demands or challenging seasons, the prospect of prioritizing oneself may seem unattainable. That's why it's essential to redefine the norm and learn to establish a foundational level of self-preservation to equip individuals with the resilience needed to navigate life's complexities.

Now, let's get into The BETTER Self Formula – a three-part strategy designed to lay the groundwork for self-preservation tailored to individual lives and needs. Here's the breakdown:

Self Necessity: These are the fundamental activities essential for survival – the bare bones of self-care.

Self Care: These are actions that enhance your ability to perform better, show up, and care for yourself beyond mere survival.

Self Indulgence: These are pleasurable activities that contribute to exuding your best self, not necessary but oh-so-desired.

Now, here's the magic equation: Self Necessity + Self Care + Self Indulgence = Self Preservation = BETTER self. What's in it for you? A better version of yourself, reduced stress, enhanced individuality, increased self-belief, improved examples for others, structured decision-making to prevent neglecting yourself, and the creation of more energy, joy, and desire for life. This formula aims to shift the balance from self-sacrifice to self-preservation, providing a guide for better caregiving.

Let me share a personal revelation with you. At 42, I found myself grappling with a disabling genetic illness and the responsibilities of raising five children, three of whom required constant care. This marked a turning point, demanding a radical shift in how I prioritized self-care. The typical neglect of one's well-being, especially as a mother to young children, was no longer sustainable.

And there it was – The BETTER Self Formula emerged from a realization that the conventional understanding of self-care was flawed. The prevailing narrative around self-care did not align with the principles of self-preservation. While the term "self-care" had been broadly propagated, its application often led to depleting activities and induced guilt rather than contributing to sustaining and preserving oneself.

So, what's self-preservation all about? It's about conserving, protecting, maintaining, caring for, safeguarding, defending, securing, and keeping alive an adequate state of quality – preparing for the long-term duration of life. Successful self-preservation requires adherence to the three-part formula: Self Necessity + Self Care + Self Indulgence.

Now, let's talk about the confusion around self-care. Social media, blogs, and workshops throw generic self-care suggestions our way – exercise more, get enough rest, eat healthier, and take time away from the kitchen. But let's be real, the term "self-care" has become a catch-all, often oversimplifying a complex and individualized concept.

Enter The BETTER Self Formula, demystifying the term "self-care" by providing clarity on the diverse aspects of self-preservation. It acknowledges that self-preservation involves more than just external activities and introduces a holistic approach encompassing self-necessity, self-care, and self-indulgence. This comprehensive understanding enables individuals to align their existing practices with a more meaningful and effective approach to self-preservation.

The first layer of the formula, Self Necessity, encompasses the daily bare necessities that keep an individual functioning—basic needs such as regular showers, dental hygiene, physical activity, water intake, and adequate sleep. Recognizing these fundamental requirements is crucial for sustaining physical and mental well-being.

Self Care, constituting the largest category, involves activities that go beyond survival, aiming to improve well-being and recharge energy. It includes daily extras that contribute to a balanced self, such as short breaks for reading, gym sessions, sufficient sleep, relaxing baths, or afternoon naps. Identifying and integrating these activities into daily routines fosters a sense of value and reinforces that life encompasses more than vocational responsibilities.

The final layer, Self Indulgence, refers to activities that are considered rich, luxurious, or expensive in terms of time, energy, or money. While these activities may not be necessary for day-to-day survival, they play a role in providing a sense of refreshment, renewal, and extra care. Balancing self-indulgence is crucial, as excessive focus on these activities can lead to burnout. Realistic and intentional self-indulgences include activities like movie marathons, time spent with friends, learning new crafts, or enjoying a leisurely reading session at a coffee shop.

Creating a personalized BETTER Self Formula involves recognizing individual circumstances, resources, and environments. While the core formula remains constant, its manifestation varies from person to person. Starting with a self-assessment based on one's Life-Season Profile, individuals can determine their unique needs, desires, and realities. A notebook serves as a valuable tool for documenting and refining the BETTER Self Formula, encompassing self-necessities, self-care activities, and self-indulgences.

Key questions to guide the customization of the formula include:

- What daily or consistent activities do I need to function effectively?
- What activities contribute to my overall well-being and help me be my best?
- What indulgences, though not essential, provide the extra care needed to reset completely?
- How do I recognize the need for self-care, and how can I incorporate it into daily life for consistent refreshment?

Creating a list of activities for each category and keeping it accessible provides a quick reference guide for moments when a lift is needed. For instance, in times of complete burnout, a solitary bubble bath may not suffice. The bath may serve as an opportunity to reflect on missing elements and devise strategies to incorporate more necessity and care into daily activities.

In essence, The BETTER Self Formula is a blueprint for enhanced self-care that transcends superficial recommendations. It offers a pathway to discover what self-preservation truly entails and guides individuals on how to refine their existing practices for a BETTER version of themselves. The formula empowers individuals to move beyond societal expectations and prioritize their well-being, fostering resilience and the capacity to thrive in the intricate dance of life.

Motherhood is overwhelming, but The BETTER Self Formula is your guide to true selflessness. Prioritize self-preservation by understanding and implementing the three components – Self Necessity, Self Care, and Self Indulgence. Transform your overwhelm into a balanced and thriving life. It's not about being perfect all the time but cultivating your BETTER, balanced self capable of withstanding life's challenges. Embrace this formula, and may it guide you toward a life of joy, energy, and self-belief.

Create your BETTER Self Formula:

- Self Necessity
- Self Care
- Self-Indulgence

About the Author

Erika Shalene Hull is an expert in Life and Business Organization Management, Author, and founder of BETTER over perfect Consulting. After spending over 10 years, primarily as a Financial Development Director for a worldwide non-profit organization, Erika sought to lessen the gap between the challenges of working and parenthood, by leaving corporate America and becoming a full-time entrepreneur. With having to overcome numerous traumas during this time, including abuse, the suicide of the oldest child, and the day-to-day hardship of a crippling genetic disorder, she is courageously passionate about helping others rise above their obstacles. From minimizing daily burdens, creating manageability, and building confidence, through BETTER over perfect, Erika provides methods, tools, and resources delivering the life fulfillment clients seek, intending to impact women's lives for the BETTER.

When she's not taking on life's challenges, she's vlogging, road

trippin', or drinking a cup of coffee with her husband and five children in Ohio.

linktr.ee/erikashalene

Chapter 10

MOMMING WITH LUSTER 101: RECLAIMING THE JOY OF MOTHERHOOD

BY ASHLEY WIZE

As a mom of ten children—my cherished four living kids and beloved son Ayzik, whom I tragically lost—I'm intimately familiar with both the magical and devastating extremes of motherhood. After teen pregnancy, single parenting, five bonus babies, twins, and losing my second-born son, Ayzik, to SIDS, I can vouch for the dizzying highs and darkest lows on the parenting rollercoaster and have weathered my fair share of tapped-out nights trying in vain for just an hour of sleep.

I spent years burying my struggles and losing myself in perfect mom mythology—to my own detriment. But, ultimately, I shifted to embracing the hilarious messiness as much as the heartwarming milestones. Now I pass on hard-won secrets so other mothers can put themselves first to fuel family joy.

In the following sections, I map out the path that's helped me and my kids thrive amidst dirty dishes, toddler meltdowns, tween angst, and my own entrepreneurial ventures. I learned how self-awareness, spirit-nurturing self-care, balanced nourishment, and chasing my dreams breed more happiness and connection than any facade of perfection. If this rescue mission to reclaim motherhood resonates, read on, and join the uprising!

SHE'S BEAUTY AND SHE'S GRACE, SHE'S MISS UNITED STATES (NOT!): EMBRACING THE MESSY AND PERFECT

As the daughter of a judgmental mother obsessed with outward "perfection," I internalized massive pressure to reflect those impossibly high standards myself—not just as a woman but especially as a new young mom. Keeping up the appearance of having it all together weighed my spirit down like a leaden cloak I couldn't shake free from. The expectation of being "on" all the darn time was the most unrealistic burden of all as I juggled twins—plus my own inner critical voice I call "Kinder." Because she behaves like a kindergartener—making big dramatic responses over small issues—but also to remind me to be kinder to myself on this imperfect parenting journey.

I distinctly remember the day my mom's harsh judgment and Kinder's inner scolding nearly crushed me: frantically tidying my home right before my own baby shower celebration while juggling rambunctious toddler twins. As my mom walked in, instead of offering relief, she scolded me over the inevitable toddler mess while I still needed to dress for guests soon arriving.

Her criticism unlocked the realization that I had to change or risk passing generational trauma down to my precious children. But transforming my mindset from perfectionist to presence-focused didn't happen overnight. I'm still actively working to reframe each chaotic moment as perfection in the making—like when I finally get the living room presentable, only to come back finding toys strewn like confetti everywhere. Or the days I meticulously tidy the car before errands, asking the kids to keep healthy snacks contained. But I inevitably still end up finding leftover wrappers tucked under seats and smashed dinner peas ground into the rug. On those hustling-to-be-on-time days, my mini tornados suddenly morph into sloths while I attempt to get kicked-off shoes back on once parked.

Isn't it funny that my most chaotic days schlepping kids from place to place also tend to deliver the most giggles and connection?

Rather than getting frustrated that my efforts got "wasted" tidying up yet again, I take a breath and proclaim: this is just the imperfectly perfect dance of motherhood. Beauty lies in embracing the spirited adventure together, crumbs and all. My graceful crown shines brighter for it.

Sometimes I do have to tell Kinder the critic to shut the entire eff up! Other times I calmly bring her back to focus and redirect, affirm, and guide her into a new place of love, assurance, and peace. It continues being a practice to confidently proclaim: I'm beautiful, I'm graceful. Flaws just make this mama's crown shine brighter!

WOKE BY WEE ONES: KIDS AS OUR SELF-AWARENESS SHERPAS

One of the most memorable instances of self-awareness dawned on me during a simple exchange with my seven-year-old daughter, Karleigh. On a typical day, I asked her to lend a hand with her baby sister, expecting her to eagerly assist. To my surprise, she calmly responded, "But Mom, you're the mom. You should handle it." Initially, her words stirred a pang of irritation within me, but the truth they carried struck deep. Karleigh's honesty served as a mirror reflecting my tendency to delegate parental duties, often sidestepping the messier aspects of motherhood. In that moment, I realized the importance of fully embracing my role, even if it meant setting aside other responsibilities.

Before diving into parenthood, I grappled with false self-perceptions rooted in shame, low self-esteem, and emotional instability. However, the arrival of my children illuminated the areas where growth was needed, particularly in cultivating kindness, patience, and grace. Their unwavering sense of justice and fairness constantly challenges me to embody these qualities, serving as gentle reminders to approach life with empathy and understanding.

Children possess an innate knack for shattering denial with their unfiltered honesty. Karleigh's candid remarks about my "shaky booty" or morning breath, though initially embarrassing, became catalysts for embracing imperfections with humor and humility. Through laughter, I learned to release unrealistic standards and embrace the beautifully messy moments of motherhood.

Becoming a mother unearthed deep-seated wounds from my own childhood, notably issues of abandonment and rejection. Explaining certain rules or boundaries to my children often triggers memories of my upbringing, where blurred boundaries and premature responsibilities were the norm. Recognizing these patterns has propelled me on a journey of healing and growth, breaking free from unhealthy dynamics.

One of the most profound sources of validation and confidence has been my children's unwavering belief in my culinary skills. Despite lingering doubts about my past, they see me as the ultimate chef, showering me with praise and admiration. Their confidence serves as a powerful reminder to trust in my abilities, fostering a sense of pride and fulfillment.

Moving forward, I aim to nurture my children's self-awareness through honest and open communication. By sharing our experiences, struggles, and triumphs, we create a safe space for growth and reflection. Through ongoing dialogue, I hope to instill in them the importance of self-awareness and personal development, guiding them toward a future filled with authenticity and purpose.

In weaving these stories together, I'm reminded of the rich tapestry of experiences that motherhood offers. It's a journey filled with laughter, tears, and countless lessons learned. I strive to share these insights with fellow mothers, embracing both the profound and the quirky moments that make this journey uniquely ours.

MOM FUEL: THE SELF-CARE SECRET TO BEING PRESENT

In the whirlwind of motherhood and entrepreneurship, self-care isn't just a luxury—it's a lifeline. For me, it's about carving out moments of peace and solitude before the chaos of the day begins. Waking up long before my children, I relish the quiet stillness of the morning, savoring a cup of tea while basking in moments of meditation and gratitude. It's a ritual that sets the tone for the day ahead, grounding me in a sense of calm and clarity.

Prioritizing self-care amidst the hustle and bustle of parenthood and running multiple businesses requires intentionality and discipline. Despite the demands of social media and the ever-present notifications, I've learned to keep my phone on sleep mode, reserving precious moments of uninterrupted focus for myself. Limiting my time on social media, despite its role in building my businesses, has been essential in preserving my mental well-being and fostering a deeper connection with myself and my loved ones.

Self-care and self-concept are intricately linked; feeling unworthy of the life you desire can lead to neglecting your own well-being while caring for others. As the oldest child, I naturally took on the role of caretaker, ensuring my mother's financial stability and providing emotional and physical support. I also became a protector for my brother, sometimes stepping in more than necessary. As a mother and wife, I was engulfed in caring for their every need, neglecting my own emotional and physical health. One day, I woke up to find everything I had worked for crumbling around me. My children were not behaving as I had hoped, my brother resented my overbearing nature, my mother moved across the country to start anew, and worst of all my partner left me. Staring at my reflection, I realized I had lost myself completely. My personal hygiene and mental well-being had deteriorated, and I was drowning in a life I no longer recognized. I knew I had to change. I understood that to feel good again, I had to look and smell good and embody the wealthy, happy, whole woman I knew I could be. It was time to prioritize myself, to fill my own cup before pouring into others. This realization marked the beginning of my journey to never lose myself in anyone else (no matter their relationship) ever again.

Yet, amidst the chaos and occasional setbacks, I refuse to succumb to feelings of guilt or hesitation when taking time for myself. Instead, I remind myself of the profound truth: I deserve the same love, time, and attention that I tirelessly give to others. By prioritizing my own self-care, I become a better version of myself—a better mother, entrepreneur, and human being.

One particularly memorable morning stands out as a testament to the transformative power of self-care. In our new home, amidst an environment infused with positivity and renewal, I found myself waking up with renewed energy and purpose. Showered, refreshed, and armed with a steaming cup of tea, I greeted the day with a sense of calm and readiness. As I tended to my children's needs with newfound patience and presence, I witnessed the ripple effects of my self-care routine. Sibling quarrels were diffused with ease, and a sense of harmony permeated our interactions throughout the day.

In the journey of motherhood and entrepreneurship, self-care isn't just a luxury—it's a necessity. By nurturing ourselves, we replenish our reserves of love, patience, and resilience, enabling us to show up fully for our loved ones and pursue our passions with renewed vigor.

KITCHEN MAGIC: CONJURING CALM FOR MOM AND BABY

In our home, the kitchen isn't just a place to prepare meals—it's our sanctuary, our haven of warmth and connection. Food is our love language, a means of nourishing not only our bodies but also our souls. As a mother and entrepreneur with a background as a chef, the kitchen plays a central role in how I nurture my children and foster a sense of togetherness within our family.

From an early age, I've delighted in exposing my children to the rich tapestry of flavors and cuisines from around the world. Thanks to countless hours spent in the kitchen, they can distinguish between the subtle nuances of ingredients—for example, discerning the difference between crab and lobster with ease. We've made a tradition of cooking together at home, immersing ourselves in the joys of homemade meals and shared experiences.

Yet, even the most cherished traditions can lose their luster over time. I'll never forget the moment when my children, weary of home-cooked fare, clamored for the convenience of fast food and takeout.

Reluctantly, I acquiesced to their requests, only to witness their swift return to the comfort of home-cooked meals within weeks. It was a poignant reminder of the irreplaceable bond forged in the kitchen—a bond that transcends the allure of convenience and novelty.

My seven-year-old son, Ahliver, has inherited my passion for cooking and eagerly joins me in the kitchen whenever the opportunity arises. With a mischievous twinkle in his eye, he'll grab a knife and cutting board, eager to concoct his culinary creations. While his enthusiasm often outpaces his caution, I take comfort in knowing that our shared love for cooking fosters not only culinary skills but also a sense of independence and creativity.

Tea, with its soothing warmth and gentle aroma, holds a special place in our hearts as a family. Bedtime rituals are incomplete without a comforting cup of tea, a ritual that imbues our evenings with a sense of tranquility and serenity. Paired with a relaxing bath and a nourishing dinner, tea time serves as a catalyst for peaceful slumber—a moment of calm amidst the hustle and bustle of daily life.

Navigating the complexities of mealtime with young children presents its own set of challenges, from accommodating allergies to managing picky eaters. Yet, through careful planning and preparation, we've found ways to ensure that mealtime remains a source of joy and connection for our family. Whether it's starting dinner preparations early in the day or meal planning for the week ahead, our efforts in the kitchen are always guided by a commitment to nourishing both body and soul.

As I reflect on my experiences in the kitchen, I'm reminded of the profound lessons and insights it has imparted. Mealtime isn't just about sustenance—it's an opportunity to deepen our connections with our children, to nourish their bodies and minds, and to create lasting memories together. By infusing our meals with love, intention, and a dash of creativity, we not only satisfy our hunger but also cultivate a sense of calm and contentment that permeates every aspect of our lives.

HAVING IT ALL BY DOING IT ALL (WELL, MOSTLY): MOM BOSSING MY WAY

Barbara Corcoran once famously said, "I gave up work-life balance the week after I had my first child at 46." And let me tell you, I feel that in my bones! Now, let's be real: achieving that elusive work-life balance often feels like attempting to juggle flaming torches while riding a unicycle. But fear not, my friends, for I've donned my super-hero cape and embarked on a quest to crack the code to this balancing "act."

First things first, let's address the elephant in the room: is it even possible to strike a harmonious chord between mom duties and entrepreneurial endeavors? Well, let's just say it's a bit like chasing a unicorn through a rainbow—magical, but not always practical. However, that doesn't mean we throw in the towel and resign ourselves to a life of chaos and caffeine-fueled desperation.

So, how do we navigate this tumultuous terrain with grace and sanity intact? It's all about creating separation of space and time, my friends. Picture this: a serene oasis where the chaos of motherhood and the demands of entrepreneurship are kept at arm's length, allowing you to savor moments of peace and calm amidst the storm.

One strategy that's been a game-changer for me is the art of prioritization. Each day, I don my CEO hat and identify the tasks that absolutely cannot wait—whether it's sealing that crucial business deal or ensuring my little ones are fed, clothed, and (mostly) happy. By focusing on what truly matters, I can navigate through the day with purpose and clarity.

Another lifesaver? Routines and schedules. I've crafted a daily roadmap that strikes the perfect balance between work and play, allowing me to carve out dedicated chunks of time for both my entrepreneurial pursuits and precious moments with my kiddos. And let me tell you, there's nothing quite as liberating as knowing exactly where you need to be and what you need to do at any given moment.

But hey, let's not forget the importance of flexibility. Life as a "mompreneur" is a wild and unpredictable ride, filled with unexpected twists and turns. So, while routines are great, it's equally important to embrace the chaos and roll with the punches—because let's face it, sometimes life throws us curve balls that no amount of planning can prepare us for.

CONCLUSION: EMBRACING THE JOURNEY OF MOTHERHOOD AND ENTREPRENEURSHIP

As I reflect on the journey of motherhood and entrepreneurship, I'm reminded of the myriad challenges and triumphs that have shaped my path. From the early days of sleepless nights and endless diaper changes to the exhilarating highs of building and growing my own businesses, each moment has been a testament to the resilience, strength, and unwavering love that defines the journey of motherhood.

Through the ups and downs, I've learned valuable lessons about perseverance, adaptability, and the power of embracing both the chaos and the calm. Motherhood has taught me to cherish the fleeting moments and celebrate the small victories, while entrepreneurship has empowered me to dream big, take risks, and carve out my own path in the world.

But perhaps most importantly, motherhood and entrepreneurship have taught me the invaluable lesson of resilience. In the face of adversity, setbacks, and challenges, I've learned to pick myself up, dust myself off, and keep moving forward with unwavering determination and belief in myself.

And as another inspirational "mompreneur," Sophia Amoruso, once said, "The most successful entrepreneurs I know are optimistic. It's part of the job description."

About the Author

Ashley Wize, aka Luster Mama, is a dedicated "mompreneur," entrepreneur, and advocate for empowering moms to thrive in both their personal and professional lives. As the founder of several successful businesses and a passionate advocate for women's empowerment, Ashley brings a wealth of experience and expertise to her work.

Ashley has become a trusted resource and mentor for women seeking to balance motherhood with their entrepreneurial dreams. Through her blog, *Momming with Luster*, Ashley shares valuable insights, tips, and strategies for navigating the challenges o f motherhood and entrepreneurship with grace and resilience.

Connect with Ashley on Facebook at Ashley Wize and on TikTok, YouTube, and Instagram @wizeandshine.

linktr.ee/wizeandshinewellness

This chapter is dedicated to all of Ashley's children: Aaron, Ayzik, Karleigh, Ahliver, Aryah, and her bonus babies, Aryan, Rob Jr., Terrik, Aryele, and Tyrell. Their love, support, and endless inspiration fuel Ashley's passion for making a positive impact in the world.

Chapter 11

EMBRACING THE HATERS AND HELPERS ON THE
JOURNEY TO MOTHERHOOD

BY RENA MCDONALD

Motherhood was an unexpected journey for me. While I always wanted children, my husband and I had both been told that we would not be able to conceive naturally. We figured we would adopt at some point in the far future. I opened my law firm in 2007 and, at the time, was focused solely on real estate clients. I was navigating the stress of starting a business when the housing market began to crash. I was very focused on my career and having a baby was far from my thoughts.

So, it was quite shocking when we discovered that we were pregnant. While, as an adult, I clearly understand how pregnancy occurs, our previous medical advice made it clear that wasn't going to happen. I was elated and scared to death. How were we going to manage the market crash, a new business, and a baby?

Now, I am an independent woman who believes, realistically or not, that I can do most things. I figured that I would be able to juggle everything and make it work. I knew that things were going to have to change both in my personal and professional lives. I was incredibly focused on what I was going to do and how I was going to juggle everything. I assumed that I would be able to handle this on my own and naïvely assumed that I would be the only one involved in either my success or failure. I began working hard on how I was going to make success happen.

What I wasn't at all prepared for was the way that other people would become such a part of the process on my journey to mother-hood. I want to be clear my child and spouse were going to be a part of the process, but I am referring to everyone else, outside of my immediate family, who shaped my journey for better or worse. I now lovingly refer to these individuals as the *haters* and the *helpers*.

THE HATERS

I would be remiss if I didn't mention all the ladies who regale you with their pregnancy horror stories the moment they find out you are expecting. They vividly describe how they almost died and suffered through hours of pain then only to comment "But it won't be like that for you." This conversation happened almost every week without fail. Ladies, why do we do this to each other? What is the point? There is no race to victory over who suffered more. Why do we heap these stories upon the first-time mother as if she wants this information? She isn't going to give you a medal, and there certainly is no prize for her. Most of these comments are meant well but often are the cause of many a first-time mother's nightmares and anxiety, which is constantly reinforced.

Now you may think I'm breaking my own advice by regaling you with my own story, but this story is not an anecdote meant to be told to a mother-to-be but rather a cautionary tale about letting others influence you into not trusting your instincts or needs.

As my pregnancy developed, I continued working on and in my firm. At first, it was just me. I had no support staff. I would drive all over town to meet with clients and get deals done. My third trimester was in the summer. We live in Las Vegas where temperatures frequently reach the 120's. To say I was hot is a complete understate-ment. I drove a Jeep Wrangler with a soft top. The roof was made of plastic and the air conditioning barely worked. This was not a problem until I was nine months pregnant driving through the Las

Vegas desert summer sun. I remember days of driving for hours and getting home and covering myself with bags of frozen vegetables to cool down. I was miserable.

Many of my clients knew I was pregnant but made very little effort to conduct business in a way that was helpful, even as a courtesy. At that time, my industry was dominated by men, and as a woman, I had to work harder for less just to be competitive. This was not just a personal belief I held as paranoia. This was a reality at that time and seemed to be reflected in the opinions of my clients.

Fortunately, we made it through the summer heat and were ready to deliver. The delivery ended up being a cesarean that was scheduled with about one week's notice. I was scheduled to go into the hospital in the evening. It was an exhausting day where every minute felt both fast and slow as if we were in some time paradox. I woke up knowing in one-half day, the baby would be here. I kept thinking, "Five hours 'til I have a baby—I'm not ready!" then, "Four hours, I can't wait," and then, "Three hours—I need more time." It was crazy. I continued to work all day trying to get last-minute emails and calls done.

Our delivery went well, and our son was beautiful. Those first moments with him were incredible. Then after they whisked him away, the nurses and doctors in the hospital started asking me legal questions *about their own personal lives* as they sewed me back up. Truly, I was a captive audience and could do nothing but answer *their* questions. Later, I was reunited with my son and my husband, and I passed out feeling so blessed and thankful.

The next day I awoke to messages from clients and other attorneys that needed immediate responses. I remember working in the hospital as the lactation specialist was trying to work with me. I had to keep asking them to give me a moment. It was overwhelming.

I turned down pain medication because I did not want to be groggy for meetings. Now you may think that some of this was just me proving a point or that I am some kind of masochist. Believe me, this behavior was the expectation of my clients and opposing attorneys. How do I know that this was their expectation? Because they told me so. I kept getting messages and phone calls telling me the same.

I vividly remember a man I worked with in a complimentary industry who referred many of his clients to me. His clients and referrals made up a large portion of my income and book of business as I was still a smaller firm. I needed to keep him happy, or I feared that it would dramatically affect my livelihood. He reminded me several times before I went into labor that he expected me to still be available for his clients.

The day after I had my son, I believe one of his messages went to voicemail. I was still in the hospital waiting for my son's test results to see if we would get discharged, but I immediately called him back. He advised that he was incredibly disappointed and that it was clear to him that I wasn't making him or his client's priorities as I "now had a child, so must be unable to get my work done." He went on to say that as a mother I was clearly distracted. Yes, I was distracted I was hooked up to IVs trying to heal after being cut in half. The pressure and demands made upon me in the hospital made my blood pressure rise and I almost didn't get released. I was avoiding pain meds and was in excruciating pain all while falling in love with a new human. It was surreal.

By comparison, I had a male friend who was also an attorney (we went to law school together); he had a similar circumstance with a completely different experience. We started our firms at about the same time and his wife became pregnant. No one expected him to work while at the hospital, and all of his clients merely congratulated him and went on with their business. When he and I discussed it later it was a huge wake-up call to me that we weren't as similar in our situations as I thought. His clients never made comments about his shifting priorities or his ability to represent them because he had a child. The expectations of a father appeared to be completely different.

I continued to struggle through the first few months of being a mother. There was nowhere to breastfeed. I would try to sit in the bathrooms at court trying to pump in between hearings, which proved nearly impossible to do. I was extremely frustrated and would often cry the whole time. Needless to say, breastfeeding didn't work out for me.

While my son was in utero it was discovered that he had a potentially small issue with one kidney. This was just an increased potential for kidney issues as he grew up, nothing conclusive or absolute. When he was born, the issue could not be conclusively identified, and future problems were all just possibilities. When we tried to include our son on our insurance plan, he was denied for having a preexisting condition. That's right, something they saw on an ultrasound once precluded him from insurance coverage. Months later, he had a high fever and my husband and I struggled with whether it was high enough that we should take him to urgent care given we knew how much that was going to cost. The system became a *hater* and caused us so much undue unnecessary stress.

I also struggled with trying to manage my life with a little one at home. It was very difficult to balance work and motherhood knowing that our family relied on my contribution to the household income; without it, we just didn't have enough. I worked a lot and often felt as if I wasn't doing enough of the other things. I felt like I wasn't there enough for my son. I couldn't hold him enough. I tried to time things so I could make phone calls while he slept and would mute myself so the people I was on the phone with couldn't hear him in the background. I judged myself and constantly found myself lacking. I became my own *hater*.

No person should ever have to go through that level of stress. Today, I would not allow this to happen to myself or anyone I care about, but then I didn't know better and thought I was doing a bad job. As I look back now, I am so sad for the mother who didn't have enough confidence to say "no" and stick up for herself.

I mention these *haters* in case you have dealt with or are dealing with something similar. My hope is that by highlighting these people and their hateful vitriol, you may find the strength to say "no" and focus on the amazing developing bond with your child and family rather than focus on what the *haters* do or think.

THE HELPERS

It took me a while to learn to stop running on this insane hamster wheel and focus on what really mattered: my family. I would be totally remiss by not mentioning the *helpers* in my life.

I am incredibly lucky to have an amazing mother who not only is willing to help but wants to be a part of my children's lives. She helped take care of them when I had to be away. To this day she continues to pick them up and help so that I can not only run a successful business but also maintain a fantastic relationship with my husband. I would never have been able to function without her.

I also am still amazed by how much more I appreciate her for being my mother as I have traveled my path of motherhood. They say you never know a person until you walk in their shoes and that couldn't be more accurate than when it comes to being a mother. My mother gave me an amazing childhood despite many challenges and obstacles. If I wanted to try playing the cello or do gymnastics, she found a way to make it happen. She was supportive in a way I didn't comprehend until I became a mother. I can appreciate her sacrifices and struggles in a new way; I thought I understood and appreciated, but I never really did until I had to make the tough decisions. She is one of the biggest and most amazing *helpers* any mother could have, and I am lucky to have her in my corner and on my list.

I also have to mention my amazing husband. He understood that having a child was a joint venture that required an equal amount of responsibility. Too often it is easy to feel like we must do everything. I was raised to believe that I could and should be able to do everything —that I could be Wonder Woman both at work and home. This is simply unnecessary. I was afraid to ask for help because I thought it made me weak. I realize now that my husband was struggling with his own journey being a father. He wanted to help but didn't always know what I needed because I wasn't communicating that. My husband and I would "split shifts" with the kids so that we each were able to get enough sleep to be semi-functional. We took turns changing diapers and making bottles. He was and is amazing.

Without him, I don't think I could have been the mother I wanted to be to our children. I wish I had recognized and appreciated him earlier on in our son's life.

Lastly, the countless friends and family who offered help along the way can't be ignored. From the friend who made us a home-cooked meal the time our house flooded and we were living in a hotel to the friend who offered to take the kids to movies one afternoon so I could finish some work, they all helped in a big way. Looking back I'm not sure we would have made it without them.

Also, the strangers who helped for no reason made me successful. I remember my son freaking out one day in Target because he wanted a toy. I had been working all day and was overwhelmed but needed to grab some groceries for dinner. I kept running into this nice lady who smiled at us in different aisles as my son's tantrum grew and grew. Finally, I couldn't take it anymore and I pulled him from the cart and left the store. The employee who took my cart from me, knowing everything would have to be put back, gave me an annoyed look as I rushed out the door. I got my son into the car and the tears just burst out. It wasn't even a big deal, but at that moment I felt like the biggest failure. Just then the nice lady walked by my car. We made eye contact, she smiled, and told me I was "doing great." It was such a simple gesture that completely changed the trajectory of my day. I got back into the car, drove to McDonalds, and got a Happy Meal and an ice cream sundae. When we got home, we played with the Happy Meal toy and snuggled for the rest of the day. On the terrible days, I would think of that amazing human and how that simple phrase made me feel. She was a *helper* who helped me on my path of motherhood.

WHY IT MATTERS

Looking back, I recognize that all these people helped shape my relationship with my children. I can recognize now that I spent way too much time focusing on the *haters* and not nearly enough time thanking the *helpers*. I know that kind words and helpful gestures mean so much more than judgment. When you first become a mother there are so many expectations—the ones we place on ourselves, and the ones others give us. All of them are unnecessary.

I was the first woman in my family to go to college and the first person to get a doctoral degree. I have been an attorney now for over twenty years and have helped countless people with their legal issues. I have owned my own law firm since 2007. I have sat on the board of many non-profit organizations and helped raise millions of dollars for the people in my community. I have written several books, and I am an international best-selling author. Having done these things, the single most important thing I have done is become a mother.

I also always thought I couldn't wait to be a mom to girls and raise empowered young women. Fate decided I had other lessons to learn and gave me two beautiful boys. I never thought I would want to be a boys' mom; I was all about girl power. But now, I realize that it couldn't be any other way. I love being a boys' mom and have discovered that I enjoy doing "boy" things. I like playing outside in the mud, camping, and fishing. My children have helped me grow and realize that I had many of my own preconceived notions that didn't stand the test of time. My children are the most amazing gift I have ever received; they are truly a blessing.

Knowing what I now understand fifteen years later, I am so thankful for both the *haters* and the *helpers* in my life. You can't appreciate the sun without the night. Motherhood is a perfect example of what it is to struggle and flourish at the same time. Motherhood is so incredibly difficult and is so rewarding.

The journey to motherhood is different for everyone. Remember to ignore the *haters* and to thank the *helpers*.

About the Author

Rena McDonald is the managing partner of Eclipse Law Group, a general civil litigation firm operating since 2007. Rena and her firm have been recognized for their achievements and have won many awards, including Top 100 Lawyers, Best of Las Vegas, Top 100 Women in Las Vegas, and Best Business For Las Vegas. Rena has also been featured in several magazines and identified as a "person to know" in Southern Nevada. Rena McDonald is committed to serving the Las Vegas community. Rena was born and raised in Las Vegas and is very involved in improving her community. Rena was also recognized by the Henderson Chamber of Commerce and other organizations for her community service efforts. Rena is a best-selling author, entrepreneur, and mother.

linktr.ee/renamcdonald

Chapter 12

IT CAN'T HAVE LANDON
BY WENDY AND SIERRA RIDDLE

I have always viewed the parenting world as somewhat of an alien adventure—an intergalactic mission where none of us have any idea of what we are getting into, and there are no manuals or instructions. Some parenting quests are like a breezy walk-through space. Mine, however, was like being pummeled with asteroids attempting to completely obliterate my little spaceship.

I should have known from the beginning of my pregnancy that the human I was going to be bringing onto this earth was a very special person: from the moment I got pregnant I started throwing up severely and could not stop. I went to the emergency room after two weeks of vomiting, thinking I had food poisoning that would not end, only to be told I was pregnant. One of my friends recommended that I get an abortion and, at that moment, something overcame me. It seemed as if time was standing still, and I heard a very loud and profound voice telling me that I had better not—and if I did, the world would suffer and be very sorry.

The vomiting continued to get even worse. I had no clue how to be a mom or what that would even look like, so I did the only logical thing I knew to do: I called my mom and made the decision to move to Utah and live with her so she could help me. We found an excellent doctor and I continued with the pregnancy. I lost twenty pounds in my first trimester of pregnancy. And I faced an onslaught of high-risk pregnancy issues throughout.

One day in the shower, my baby started kicking very violently in a downward motion towards my vagina and would not stop. I felt a very sharp pain and then a jellyfish-looking creature came out of me. I scooped it into a bag and rushed to my doctor's office. Where he told me that was my mucus plug. And I was now about to go into early labor—five weeks early! The doctor wanted to admit me, but being as stubborn as I am, I wanted to go home and get all my things and then check into the hospital.

I was admitted to the hospital and I was given Pitocin, a medication to force dilation. And once I was dilated by nine centimeters, I was told I was going to be pushing for hours until delivery. I looked that doctor directly in his face and told him that my baby was coming out now and if he let my child fall on the floor he would be the next one on the floor!! I pushed two times and Landon Marcello came right out. There was a huge shock in the room at that moment—Landon's umbilical cord was wrapped twice around his neck and had a knot in it, but he was fine and healthy! The doctor proclaimed loudly, "This child forced himself to be born to save his own life!" About two days later, I woke up from the whole ordeal and was expecting my son to be in the NICU; however, I was quite shocked when he was right beside me and they told me he was ready to go home before I was. They told me that he was perfectly healthy, even being a premature baby! So, home we went!

The next two years were the calm before the storm of our lives. At times it is honestly hard for me to remember what Landon was like before...what our life was like before the storm. But I do remember him being a very happy baby, hitting all his milestones ahead of time, and being so full of life and energy that it was quite difficult to keep up with him! He was zooming! I always joked that Landon went straight from crawling to running. At two and a half years old he, was fifty pounds of solid muscle and healthy as could be!

In early September of 2012, I was in Georgia and my mom and

Landon's godparents were taking care of him. Landon's godparents took him to a regular checkup appointment and were told he needed his MMR vaccine. Thinking, like most people, that it was no big deal, they agreed, and my son received his vaccination. In less than thirty days Landon became ill. He was coughing and had a slight sore throat; he had no fever or other issues, but his godparents took him to the doctor to get him checked out. The medical professionals pricked his finger, ran the blood, and reported that he was fine and that it was just a virus. The cough continued to get worse, so my mom took him back again and they did the same finger-prick blood test and assured her that he was fine. A few days later he was at his godparents' house for a sleepover and when they went to change his diaper, the lymph nodes in his groin were huge and swollen. They tried to reach my mom, but she was in the shower, so they just took him to the hospital. They picked up my mom at her house and took her to the hospital. When my mom arrived at the hospital, the hospital staff told her that the blood work and x-rays had come back and he had leukemia. She was certain that they were wrong, but no such luck. They had already contacted the children's hospital in Salt Lake City and were preparing to airlift him and my mom.

In the blink of an eye, my son was swarmed with multiple doctors as well as flight nurses and PICU nurses prepping him for the flight. My mother described the scene once the jet landed as organized chaos—there were twenty-six doctors and medical professionals waiting for her and my son. They jumped in and started all the testing and reported that Landon only had a 10% chance of surviving the next 24-48 hours. My mom called me in Georgia to tell me what was going on and, in the blink of an eye, my world changed forever. The doctors reported that if I wanted to see my son before he died, I needed to get to Salt Lake City (SLC) immediately. My mom called her dear friend Dawn, who jumped in and got me to the airport to fly to SLC.

I am truly not sure how I got through that day—or any of the days that followed for the next few long torturous months—other than through the grace and strength of God and my mother because I was a royal wreck. How could my son have **terminal cancer?!** How did he get it? Is he going to live? What caused this?? How do you even go about trying to plan a funeral for a two-year-old who was completely healthy and now about to die from cancer?! My mind raced in every direction known to man...But the one thing I did know—and I knew it deep down in my bones and in my soul—was that I was not going to let my son die!! No matter the cost and no matter the consequences.

Once you get the "lottery ticket" of having a child with cancer, your life is completely changed and over as you knew it. This is a hard reality to accept—yet, at the same time, it has already changed from the day you hear those words: **"Your child has cancer."**

The next few weeks were all spent in Salt Lake City at Primary Children's Hospital and Huntsman's Cancer Institute. Landon began immediate chemotherapy and then radiation. The effects were devastating.

Within ninety days Landon had lost 50% of his body weight. He lost his ability to walk directly due to Vincristine, a chemotherapy drug. He lost his ability to eat and was IV-fed. He developed severe nausea and was vomiting upwards of twenty-five to fifty times per day. He was prescribed very dangerous narcotics such as morphine and oxycontin...all at only two years old. He had chemical burns on his rear from the chemo. The side effects of these narcotics were also devastating. Landon would pick his skin incessantly; he developed night terrors as well as PTSD and paranoia. It was a real-life nightmare and horror movie. Landon needed multiple blood and platelet transfusions, as the chemotherapy was destroying every cell in his body.

In January 2013, Landon was life-flighted due to a severe virus mixed with his already horrific conditions from chemotherapy and radiation. At this point, my mother, Wendy, and I had already been looking for something...anything that could help save my son's life that would kill the cancer but not him since, clearly, that is what the chemotherapy and radiation were doing.

That Life Flight was the last straw for us.

As we sat and listened to Landon's oncology team tell us he was in critical condition **from their treatments** and his body needed at least a two-week rest from chemo as his body could take no more...well, that was the end for this family. We were told to return home with Landon, that nurses would come in to check on and care for him daily until his body recovered, or he expired, as those were truly the only two options available. We left that hospital and went in the opposite direction.

That changed all our lives forever.

We decided to try something else...something so controversial that my mom and I could go to prison for trying...simply to attempt to save my son's life. But I had already decided that no matter the cost or consequences, my son was going to live. My mom had been looking into cannabis for over a month, but there were no other kids who had used cannabis for cancer. There were no parents to talk with, there were no case studies to read, and there was zero proof that this would work or even help him. My mom called several doctors who did recommend cannabis for adults, and they reported that they did not know if it would work, but they all reported that it **would not hurt him**. The chemo was killing him, so what did we have to lose??

"Saving Landon Riddle" is the next chapter—release date July 2024.

About the Author

Sierra Riddle, the founder of www.cbdforall.org, has earned the title of "OGCannaMom" and a reputation as a cannabis pioneer. Sierra is fighting to cure and heal her two-year-old son, cancer and cannabis warrior Landon Riddle, while also running a nonprofit that helps a nation of people fighting cancer with cannabis oils. This serial entrepreneur has created multiple brands in the cannabis space but is most recently known for her role as the "Mushroom Maven" in the emerging new market of psychedelics. Nationwide news coverage of the controversial fight she had with Child Protective Services (CPS) over her son's cancer treatment and insistence on using cannabis oils instead of chemotherapy shook the world!

She's a female Robinhood, an expert in multiple areas of plant-based medicine treatments, creates custom cancer protocols, is a branding and formulation specialist, and has significant knowledge in cannabinoid medicine and science. She started Landon's Health Hut to bring attention to her son's successful battle against leukemia, which  caught the world's attention and created a ripple effect seen and felt worldwide.

linktr.ee/OGCannaMom

Chapter 13

A FITNESS JOURNEY THROUGH TIME
BY AUDRA ROMEO

I walk into the gym around 5:00 p.m. and head to the small studio where I teach my HIIT class.

Damn, I'm so tired. Traffic was awful. Seems like this state is getting more crowded every day.

I plop down my gym bag on the floor and eyeball the studio to make sure all the equipment is where it needs to be for today's class. Oh good, the benches are out. I have about five minutes before some of the class members come in. I go to the back of the studio and lay down on one of the benches just to decompress from that hour-long drive from work.

After a few minutes, I get up, feeling slightly more energized, and I take my place on one of the treadmills to start power walking.

Once all my class participants come in and begin warming up, I check the clock. It's 5:30. I grab my mic, turn up the jams and "it's showtime!"

At the end of our 50-minute class, I'm feeling good, as is my class. The stress of our day is now a faint thought. I bid goodnight to them. I love teaching my class. Who knew that at age 57, I'd be a personal trainer, in the gym, teaching HIIT classes?

Flashback to sometime in the mid to late 70s. I'm in gym class in junior high. I hated gym class with a passion. I wasn't active by any stretch of the imagination. Plus, I wasn't the slimmest either—chubby kind of sums it up. Shy, too—did I mention that? So, with those three things going for me and the not-so-nice names I was called by some of those nasty boys, needless to say, I hated gym. Forty-odd years later, those names still sting.

In my late teens and 20s, I found aerobics. It was becoming popular in the 80s thanks to the movie *Flashdance*. So, with my big hair and leg warmers I joined a women's-only gym that offered aerobics classes. I found the class to be a lot of fun as I learned the moves while listening to my favorite songs playing over the speaker. Oddly enough, I didn't feel awkward when I messed up the steps.

During my college years, I was also playing racquetball. It was fast-paced and a great workout. It was also a great distraction from schoolwork and a stress reliever during exams.

As the years passed, my life changed, as did my fitness routines. I was doing step classes during my pregnancy with my daughter. It was a pretty easy pregnancy, so I was able to do those classes up until a week before she was born.

I took an eight-week leave of absence from work and working out. I was naturally losing the baby weight, but I missed going to class; it was my getaway. My getaway from the house and from being a new mom with new responsibilities. Don't get me wrong: I loved my baby girl, but hey, you need a break.

I went back to my step class once a week. I definitely had mom guilt as I drove to the gym. I would tell myself that it's fine, she's with her dad. He can have her for two hours—I was with her all day. I told myself that class was a relief, especially on days when she was really fussy and I was frazzled. At least when I came back, I felt better able to handle what she had in store for me for the rest of the night.

As my daughter grew, she, too, was a little chubby—not as bad as me, but I still wanted to ensure she wasn't going to be a target of ridicule in school like I was.

By the time she was six years old, I had her in dance class. I thought it would be a good way for her to be active and have an activity she may enjoy. My Saturdays were dedicated to getting her to class and watching her practice for her performances.

I enjoyed watching her learn her steps and routines, picking out costumes, getting hair and makeup done, and how the entire show came together at the end of the season.

While she spent those years doing her dances, I was still doing my "dances" on the gym floor. I was a single mom during those years, so being at the gym really helped me get through some emotional times as we had to transition to a different family unit.

We did the dance scene for a few years. Eventually, she didn't want to do it anymore, and that was okay with me. I do have to admit I really did miss Saturdays sitting in the little waiting room with all the other moms—two of whom became really good friends of mine —and watching the girls practice.

The years came and went. Divorce happened, a new relationship happened, and a relocation across the country from New York to Arizona happened. Then, at age 42, my son happened.

I was monitored throughout the whole pregnancy because of my age. Thankfully, everything went well. He came in, or should I say out, at a whopping nine pounds, 10 ounces. His head was too big, and while I was pushing he would go into distress. This went on for hours. The decision was made to perform a C-section.

I was not happy. I cried the whole time—during the procedure and after. Of course, once the nurse brought him to me I was fine.

Well, this time around the baby weight didn't come off as fast as when I had my daughter. Granted, I was in my 40s, and the C-section was a whole other experience. I couldn't go right back to working out. I didn't have a gym membership at the time because we were new to Arizona. Plus, we were too busy building up our business.

I really couldn't even walk far without feeling like my insides were going to fall out. It was a rough time both mentally and physically. I was tired, I was hurting, I had no friends, I hated the way I looked in the mirror.

It was quite a while before I finally said, "Screw this, I have to do something." I had some Tae Bo tapes, so I popped them in the VCR, put my son in his swing chair, and started working out in the living room. Baby steps.

I was starting to feel better. I was getting my energy back. I still didn't get to the weight I wanted to be, but at least I was doing something. Again, baby steps. At some point, I put my son in the stroller and walked around the neighborhood. In the evenings and weekends, my daughter joined us, along with our dog. I truly enjoyed our walks. We talked and we laughed; it was our bonding time.

Once my daughter began high school, she joined the band as color guard. I was glad she did because it got her involved with an activity, and it made her high school experience memorable in a good way rather than a bad way.

Here I was again, running to practice—this time with a toddler in tow—five days a week. Fridays were especially long during football season, but they were fun. It was just like *Friday Night Lights*; there I was sitting in the bleachers, watching high-school football with my daughter and her band members to my far right, and my son in his stroller in front of me.

I'd watch her as she and her fellow color guard and band took to the field during halftime and performed. I was in awe of how she was able to swing that six-foot flag, toss it in the air, and catch it. You go, girl! I couldn't do it!

Practices didn't stop after football season. Competition season began straight away. More Saturdays.

Those were even more fun than football. I loved watching them compete against other high schools and comparing their performance against all the others and at the end waiting for the results.

Those times will never be forgotten.

My son started playing flag football by the time he was six years old. Six seems to be the magic number.

And yet again, there I was heading out on Saturdays for practices and football games. And there I was all momma-proud, watching him catching the ball and running for touchdowns. Flag turned to tackle once he got older.

For six seasons we went to practices and games—getting up before the sun, driving sometimes over an hour away to play. I watched him grow from a little six-year-old who was afraid to catch the ball to a very talented athlete who worked hard at his game. He truly loves the game of football. I truly love the game of football.

And just as I sat and proudly watched my daughter on the football field doing her performance as a member of the band, I now sit on the sidelines watching my son on the football field doing his performance as a member of the football team. *Friday Night Lights* the second time around.

Throughout being a mom supporting my kids in their sporting endeavors, I decided I needed to do something in health and fitness. I mean, I had been working out for thirty-six years, whether it was in the gym, aerobics and step classes, or at home with videos. Plus, I really like sharing my knowledge with others and having them use that knowledge in their own lives.

I never in a million years thought about being a personal trainer. I felt like I didn't look the part. I wondered who the heck I was at 54 thinking I could become a trainer. I took a chance: I signed up for an online certification with ISSA and began my course.

My daughter and I were, at the time, going to one of the local big box gyms. I was pretty friendly with the manager there and mentioned that I was getting my certification. She told me once I was finished to just let her know and she'll put me on the schedule. Needless to say, I was surprised. Wow, no interview, nothing. Just get the certification and start.

And so began my side hustle career as a trainer and HIIT instructor doing both in-person and online training, which I offer with a training app. The app is great because I can set up a variety of workouts according to my clients' goals, plus I can still be their accountability partner by monitoring workouts and encouraging them with daily motivational messages.

Fitness developed my body, my mind, and my personality over

the years. Those first aerobics classes brought me slightly out of my shell. I was determined to know the routines so I wouldn't look like a complete fool in the back of the class. Eventually, I moved to the front of the class as I built confidence.

The classes kept my mind from thinking I was that chubby child as I slimmed down and actually didn't mind looking in the mirror.

When I wasn't gym- or class-bound, I was exercising at home. I used the VHS tapes and even walked the neighborhood with the kids and dogs. I may not have been looking or feeling my best, but the sheer simplicity of walking with them took my mind off my troubles.

Having the confidence to get certified and teach in a gym was amazing. I had so much knowledge from all those years that I would put my clients' programs together on the fly. They never have a boring workout because I have so much to offer.

The best part: they learn! It came to a point where I would ask them to lead the workout—and they would. I had done my job.

As moms, we give all we have to make sure our family is taken care of, without a lot of thought about our own needs. We're tired, we're grumpy, our bodies hurt, and we have brain fog.

I was, too. But exercise helped me through it all. As it did with menopause. I honestly believe that both of my pregnancies went well as did the recoveries. I know it was harder with the C-section, but I feel it could have been much worse.

Working out assists us with being the strong women we are. As new moms, as moms with teens, as empty nesters, as we go through menopause and beyond.

Exercise helps with it all.

You wish you had more energy. Exercise increases energy. I'm going from 6:30 in the morning all the way until 9:00 p.m., and most weekends are filled with activity. As a mom with an athlete son, there are practices and games.

Don't get me wrong, there are plenty of days I just want to sit on the couch wrapped in a blanket and binge-watch Netflix. Confession: I do once in a while.

You wish you could keep up with the kids. Exercise increases endurance.

Your back, hips, neck, and knees hurt after playing with the kids. Exercise helps prevent injury and increases strength and flexibility.

It's never too late to begin any type of exercise. My exercise journey began in junior high school thanks to being called names because I was fat. I used fitness to lose weight as a teen and twice as a new mom. I also feel that the reason I didn't have menopause symptoms was because of being active.

Now exercise is my go-to when life is stressful, when I have a bad day at work, or when my husband and I have had an argument. The best part of all is that I can help others who come to me for those very same reasons or whatever other motivation they have.

And because fitness was and still is a big part of my life, I want to give back to my fellow moms.

Ladies, let's stop being so selfless. Give yourself time for yourself, whatever your "why" may be.

About the Author

Audra Romeo is a certified personal trainer with additional certifications in exercise therapy, nutrition, and yoga, allowing her to tailor comprehensive programs that address both physical fitness and overall well-being. Audra also holds a BS in business, management, and finance and a health coach certification from INN; she combines her business knowledge with her fervor for fitness to offer a holistic approach to personal training and HIIT coaching.

Her commitment to sharing knowledge and inspiring others extends beyond one-on-one sessions; Audra is a contributing writer for *OM Yoga* magazine, where she shares insights and tips on holistic health practices.

Leveraging the power of technology, she offers online tailored personal training programs and nutrition coaching to ladies looking to unlock their full potential both physically and mentally with an empathic and enthusiastic approach.

Audra currently lives with her family, three dogs, one cat, and a tortoise in Phoenix, AZ.

To learn more about online personal training and/or nutrition coaching please visit www.formindandmuscle.com. For a free two-week workout, check out linktr.ee/audraromeo.

Chapter 14

CAN'T FIX IT
BY FRANCES TREJO-LAY

August 13, 2001

I find myself suddenly standing...no, leaning way over...on top of one of those clear, plastic maternity hospital bassinets. My hand is outstretched, hovering over my baby's sleeping body. I am about to scoop him up...Instead, I freeze. I listen, my body tense—on high alert! *What's wrong? How can I fix it?*

"Never wake a sleeping baby," pops into my head from some deep, dark memory.

I straighten up. Step back. I blink a few times. *How did I get here? I must have gotten out of bed...Am I sleepwalking? Sleep-protecting? Ah...I'm in "fight mode," like a Momma Bear.*

I look at my baby son, less than twenty-four hours old, sleeping soundly in his little fishbowl of a bassinet. He makes a little snuffling noise, reaches a little hand up and suddenly out! It startles him because he's used to the womb walls being there, keeping him safe. Miguel gives a little sigh and settles back into his deep sleep.

I push my long, dark hair out of my face and roll it into a messy bun with the black scrunchie I find on my wrist.

My heartbeat is slowing down. My rational mind slowly coming back "online."

I'm realizing that baby Miggs must have made a little sound in his sleep. It wakes me, launching me into action.

I take some deep, deep breaths, stretch, and crawl back into bed. More deep breathing, soothing my nerves in this body still coursing with hormones.

I fall back asleep, occasionally waking up throughout the night, whenever my baby makes little noises. At least now, I only open my eyes and listen. I still tense up a lot, but at least I stay in bed.

It is not quite sunrise when Miggs cries and I pick him up. I hold him close and get down to the business of "mothering."

I was twenty-nine when my son was born.

When I found out I was pregnant, I did everything to prepare for our son's arrival. I read lots of books but only one gave me a *real woman's perspective* on pregnancy and labor. What I needed was to talk to other pregnant women and brand-new mothers. At the time, there were no resources available to this newly pregnant American in Australia. Australia has fantastic medically based resources for mothers and babies, but they are available **after** your baby is born. So, I created my own mother's group for expats, just like me. (You can read more about this adventure in "Pregnant, Seeking Sisters" in *Sanctuary*, also published by Red Thread Publishing in 2022.)

In 2000-2001, as much as I prepared—as much as we all prepared for it– motherhood is still full of surprises. I expected to fall in love with my little boy, but I did not expect that almost feral instinct to take over my rational mind. I mean it was potent, this drive to fight/ maim (kill?) any threat to my newborn.

Thankfully, Momma Bear becomes less intense over time. Momma Bear becomes a "voice" in my head warning me of **potential** dangers. Luckily that coincided with our return to the USA in 2003.

And surprise! Momma Bear's voice isn't the only "voice" that impacts my parenting. All the advice and pressure from society and family; from doctors and midwives; from child-rearing "experts;" teachers and my own history and personality become "voices" that influence who I am as a woman and the mother I am **becoming**.

Even now, with twenty-two years of living in Motherland, all these "voices" still compete with each other in my head when it comes to "mothering" my adult son *properly*.

Especially in times of crisis.

❦

October 2023

The week before we are supposed to travel from California to visit Rick's mom, he wakes up with foot pain. My husband can barely walk and suspects it's plantar fasciitis. By Thursday, he calls me to his office and we phone his sister.

Rick runs an open hand from the top of his head, all the way to the nape of his neck. After twenty-six years of marriage, I recognize this gesture as a sign he is stressing out. Time is an issue because my mother-in-law was diagnosed with Lewy Body Dementia in June of 2021.

"I can't get on a plane tomorrow," he says.

"I'm sorry to hear that you are in pain, brother," my sister-in-law's soothing voice is coming from the speakerphone. "If you can't travel, you can't travel."

"You think Mom will be okay? I mean, how late is too late to come?" Rick asks.

"I don't know. I mean, with Lewy Body there is no exact way of knowing." replies his sister. Slowly, thoughtfully she continues. "I'm just concerned that she won't recognize you **at all** if you come in January. It's October now; there is the holiday traffic to take into account."

Rick says, "Mom's condition is **that** advanced?"

"Yes, Mom's staring off into space for longer and longer periods of time. And you know that when she speaks it rarely makes sense. But, it's her body's deterioration that is most concerning to me. The stoop in her neck is really bad. I was really stunned by how she looked the other day. Let me send you a picture."

We hear a familiar "swoosh," as the photo arrives on our phones in the group text we use to keep up with news of my mother-in-law.

I see Chela sitting in her wheelchair upright with her back stick straight, parallel to the backrest. But her head is bent forward in a stoop from the neck at a 175-degree angle; Chela's head hangs down, chest-level. It's like her upper body is curling into her chest—almost like taking a fetal position. Her arms loosely hug her midsection.

I am astonished by what I see. In the few seconds it takes us to study the picture and ask a question, my mind races:

This is Chela?

I don't see the Chela who traveled to Rome with me, my mother, and Janice to see Pope Benedict XIV.

*Where is the woman who took off in search of some religious souvenirs she **had** to buy when her daughter explicitly told her to stay with my mom, near a specific group of stores? Was this the woman we couldn't find for a couple of hours? The woman who, ironically, was also terrified of being lost and alone in a foreign country?*

Where is the Chela who drove my husband crazy with "her drama" each and every visit?

Where is the woman who loved it when I told her to stop cleaning and come sit with me, so I could serve her a plate of juicy chicken and white rice, with the crispy rice "concolón" that I saved just for her?

Where is the woman who loved me because I spoke Spanish and "took care of" her son, her "chinito?"

We are all worried that Chela is at death's door. We need to get there ASAP.

"Is she in pain?" Rick asks.

"It's very painful for her. Some days it's so bad and she doesn't want anyone moving her. As you can see, the Memory-Care staff are putting lidocaine patches on Mom's neck for the pain."

I feel my chest and shoulders tighten. Inside it feels like my heart is shriveling around the edges, becoming smaller, denser, and harder somehow—hardening to handle this trip to visit Chela as a family.

I wonder how this photo of Chela is affecting my husband and sister-in-law.

I mean, Chela is their **mother.**

How do I get my husband through this?

And what about Miguel? How is he going to handle this?

Miguel is only nine when, in 2010, my dad has emergency surgery. Over time my father gets better. My son never sees or hears any of the gory details. For all intents and purposes, hope and a lot of tender love and care "fixed" Grandpa Ricardo.

Our son's only experience with death is when our dog Shelby dies in May 2020. She was our fifteen-year-old chi-weenie. During the Covid-19 lockdown, all the local vet offices were closed, and Miguel is crushed to witness Shelby dying slowly, struggling to breathe. He misses her deeply.

This time it's his Grandma Chela. And she will get worse and worse until she dies.

How do I fix this?

November 2023

Rick's foot heals in roughly a week, and we reschedule our visit for three weeks later.

During this time, I can feel the tension in my body, and I am hearing all those "competing" voices in my head while trying to figure out how to fix this for my son—for my entire family.

A big part of my personality is to jump into action whenever and wherever I am needed. It is this powerful force within me. Whenever there is a crisis, I'm energetically waiting and watching for signs of what I can do to make things better. Just like that first Momma Bear moment at the hospital, I am frozen and listening... I'm waiting, taking in information so that I know what to do. But in this kind of crisis, there is literally **nothing to do.**

Watching someone go through a life-threatening condition is hard on everyone. I can see that Rick is tense. I'm agitated because my hands are tied. I am not a doctor and I can't cure Chela. I cannot shield my husband and son from the pain of watching Chela's body deteriorate. I cannot protect my son from facing the heart-breaking decline of a woman who loves him so intensely, just because he exists —just because Miguel is Chela's only grandchild.

It's obvious Miguel is really uncomfortable when he tries to get out of going with us. He tells us that he is at a crucial point in his video-game mod-development project. Even though my heart and mind are at odds with each other, we tell our son the truth.

I say, "Someday you will experience loss, again. You lost Shelby and it hurt. Well, someday someone much closer to you will die. You need to learn how to handle that. And you might as well do it with your family to help you through it."

Miguel looks thoughtful, "I know."

I continue, "Grandma Chela is still alive. It's uncomfortable for us to see her like that. But we put that aside because she needs us. She may not be able to talk to us or recognize us half the time, but she can feel our love. Our presence will mean a lot to her, in the moment. And that is what matters."

And out of my own mouth, I say and hear what I need to hear. **What matters most is our presence in the moment.** It's a couple more days before what I say to my son hits home for me. The human side of me is still too busy freaking out to allow it to fully sink in. But I'm sure my subconscious hears it because I start to lean into my strengths.

I am an intuitive Reiki healer and women's circle facilitator. I teach women how to hear their own intuition, their inner knowing, through the **deep listening** created in the sacred and safe space of a women's circle.

At fifty-two, you could say I have been working on myself for almost a lifetime. But it has been my participation in women's circles and other women-only spaces that has provided me the ability to hear my own intuition.

However, I am still very much a flawed human being. No amount of spiritual work, Reiki, meditation, intention setting, singing, ecstatic dance, yoga, or journaling will make my flaws disappear. It's actually not the point of the work. I know this from experience. Old patterns of behavior emerge, over and over again, and are especially potent during life-changing events.

Nowadays, I can spot the limiting behaviors and work **with** them. When I notice I am "spinning out," I know that my mind is stuck in a loop, fixating on a few thoughts and feelings. In my case, I suppress the feelings first. It's the normal response to stress in all humans: fight, flight, freeze, or fawn. Except for me, I can get stuck in "freeze," where I am waiting to pounce and I am numb. To shift my energy out of "freeze mode," I take the following steps:

1. **Get out of my head and back into my body.** I move. I walk or dance. I often "walk-and-talk"—speaking and voice recording my thoughts **as** I walk. It's journaling and moving at the same time.

2. **I talk to someone else.** I talk to a friend or a mentor who offers **deep listening:** they let me speak without interruption, without advice, and without trying to fix me. They know I have my own inner wisdom and I just need to voice my thoughts, hear them, and be witnessed to work through them. I go to a women's circle weekly, so many times I share these thoughts in the circle.

3. **I clarify what I am feeling.** Talking, journaling, and **deep listening** help me figure out what feelings I'm feeling.

4. **I allow myself to feel my feelings and release them.** This one is tough for me. I am an expert at holding in my feelings, especially in a crisis. Anger comes easiest. It takes

a little coaxing to allow these feelings to "be." Once I do, though, they can be easily released.

5. **I lean on my spiritual practices, tools, and gifts to discover the insights or messages I need.** What's the lesson here? Is there a lesson? Sometimes it is crystal clear. Sometimes it's as subtle as a whisper.

6. **I ask myself, "How do I want to feel?" And I check in with a friend or mentor for clarity.** Throughout this spiritual-awakening journey, I've gotten to know some fabulous, like-minded and wise women. I seek their help and book a session with them to gain some clarity. Sometimes it's just a conversation to see if my understanding rings true. They know the authentic me and can help me discern if my actions are aligned with who I am.

So, in the days before our trip, I have been going through my process. When I get to number five, it occurs to me that although I have been sending distance Reiki to my mother-in-law, it's time for a neutral party to help me with discernment.

I recognize I'm tired and I'm not "hearing the lesson" in all of this for me. I book a distance Reiki healing session with Cami, a Reiki/energy healing mentor. I trust that a session with two practitioners is more powerful than my working alone. I'm so glad I do this because I experience such soothing comfort and witness a beautiful healing.

For some practitioners and masters of the energy-healing arts, there are intuitive gifts that emerge or become stronger the more we practice energy-healing. Both Cami and I "vision": we see images, colors, and symbols that we interpret for meaning. Cami also feels what others feel during a healing.

What Cami and I both see and feel during this session brings me closer to Chela than I have ever been. I see and feel many things during this healing session that are moving, empowering, and very personal. I would need a whole other chapter to describe everything. What is more important, is **sharing the message** I "saw and heard."

I feel Chela's presence strongly. Cami and I see her as she sees herself—radiant, glowing, walking tall, in peak health, with her hair and nails done just the way she likes. I leave the session knowing that Chela is supported and protected by hundreds of her ancestors and by the spiritual beings she loves and prays to. And that they will be with her until the day she dies. I am happy knowing **Chela feels this support all around her.** More importantly, we feel Chela's overwhelming sense of joy.

On the flight to see her, I am still searching within, who should I "be?" For myself, for Chela, and for my family in this difficult situation?

I am sitting alone, behind "my boys" on the plane. I am remembering the Reiki experience and my memories of Chela before dementia, as I start a "Cosmic Smash Book" page. It is the intuitive, spiritual practice I lean on when I need clarity and my intuition isn't automatically brimming with insights.

"Cosmic Smash Booking" is a form of art-journaling created by artist Catt Geller. It is designed to reveal to us what our intuition is "saying."

I am working and praying for guidance for about twenty minutes. *Who do I need to be?* I am lost in the moment, about to pick up a dark green marker, when I feel a familiar presence. And hear, "Ese no, ¡está feo! The bright green is prettier." I smile because I feel the same energy I feel when Cami and I sent Chela distance Reiki. And I recognize my mother-in-law's word choice and tone in my head.

I ask Chela, "What do you need?" and she says, "See me as a whole person."

Now I **know** what to "do"....Or rather, who to "be."

This **knowing** brings calm. Without fear, there is clarity.

I am less worried about how my family is going to be affected.

We are all adults, and we are going to handle this the best way each of us knows how. My son and husband have their own journey and lessons to learn, in their own way and in their own time.

Momma Bear cannot protect them from their lessons.

It is not about what I am doing. It's who I choose to "be" moment to moment.

So, I chose to love and honor Chela—and my family—and trust that they feel it.

About the Author

Frances (Frankie) Trejo-Lay is a Women's Circle Facilitator. She helps women reconnect to their own intuition. By teaching **deep listening** in the sacred space of Women's Circle, women "hear" their own inner voice with clarity and rediscover the joy of manifesting their heart's deepest desires.

She is also an Energy worker offering Distance Reiki/Energy work to friends and family. She looks forward to offering intuitive and energy work to clients in the near future. Frankie is a published author with Red Thread Publishing, contributing to four anthologies: Sanctuary (2022), Planting the Seed (2023), By the Light of the Moon (2024) and Motherland (2024).

Frankie speaks Spanglish at home with her husband and adult son in the Southern California Desert. They want a dog soon. Please subscribe for links to: register for the next Community Women's Circle and for new offerings.

linktr.ee/frances_trejo_lay_SacredSpace

Chapter 15

THE STICK & THE VINE
BY SIERRA MELCHER

I didn't always dream of being a mother. In fact, well into my 30s the thought still made me shudder.

How glad I am that motherhood found me anyway. Nothing prepares you for motherhood. There's no certification or qualification. You could read the countless books on parenting but you're still going to have to figure it out for yourself. And we all mess it up.

Not Enough: A common theme I hear among parents & fellow authors alike. We hold ourselves to impossibly high standards and beat ourselves up about so much. The cultural pressure to be perfect is so instilled in us we self-enforce and suffer. For writers, this pressure usually leads to writer's block. For parents, this pressure leads to even taking on more and stressing everyone out.

The day I gave birth to my daughter I had a couple of realizations. **One:**

I was not somehow imbued with superhuman skills. I was still just me; just as lost and confused as I had always been. This realization rippled in time and space; in that instant, I discovered compassion and understanding for my parents who were just kids when I was born and didn't know what the hell they were doing either. They just did the best they could.

Two:

I was going to screw it up. I was going to fail, one way or another, in raising this incredible, tiny human that had just come into my life. Don't get me wrong, I was going to do my damnedest. I was going to do the best that I could, whether I knew how or not: to love her fiercely, protect her unabashedly, give her enough space to figure out who she is in this world, and support her to find her own way.

But I knew unequivocally that I was going to fail at something, one way or another. She'd probably need therapy. There'd surely be something that she could never forgive me for. To my surprise, *that was a relief.* The inevitable failure of parenting somehow gave me permission to *try.* Releasing the goal of perfection and the pressure of *"doing it right"* but doing my best and messing it up felt amazing. Precisely where I felt my parents failed was where I began. It's where I grew and learned most, where I figured out the most important things in my life.

With any luck, my failings will teach my daughter even more than my successes. They'll empower her to distinguish herself, to stand outside of any shadow I may cast and to fully become her own person and discover her journey.

I am going to give it my all. I will fail at this & I have come to peace with that.

I followed the thought to its logical conclusion: what it would look like if, in some imaginary fiction, I could be a flawless parent and get everything right. If I never failed and she never learned how to do it on her own: that would be the worst thing I could do. I didn't want that for myself or my daughter. I accept the fact that I will screw this up one way or another because that's where she will learn and grow. I have a few hunches already about where the cracks may exist. Life is funny. Maybe her perception of my biggest failures will be where I least expect them.

NOT QUALIFIED TO BE A PARENT

What does being a mother even mean?
How can I possibly?
When I'm just a person trying to figure out how to be me?
I don't even know where to start.
Most of the time I still feel like a teenager myself.
How can I be solely responsible for the shaping of another
human?

So much of parenting is about just keeping them fed, clean, combed, brushed, dressed, and to school on time. For thousands and thousands of days on end.

Parenting is so much more than that.

It's about helping someone figure out how to be a person. How do you help someone figure out how to be themselves?

All the time and effort I devote to this impossible task is going to just be a few core memories when she's grown. Every decision I agonize about will be a blur or non-existent for her. So what is it to be a mom and why are we so hard on ourselves?

For example, I just spent most of the holiday season trying so hard to create family traditions to make the season special. I had a ridiculous expectation of a completely tech-free three weeks. Instead, I rearranged the furniture so we could watch tons of movies on the wall. Then I felt guilty about it, feeling a "good mom" would have better activities to engage and challenge her child. Then I realized I love film; it is something I get to enjoy and share with my kid. Also, my favorite traditions are not ones I have to strive for, they are the things we do naturally... Like having a live potted tree for Christmas and advent scavenger hunts, going out to breakfast, and walking the dog to the park.

I am always behind the curve: when she was a baby she'd grow into a new developmental phase every six weeks. It would take me about eight weeks to catch up. Now she's almost nine and it's the same. I have no idea how to do this. She asks a million questions I don't know how to answer, not just the basics like "When will I get my period?" and "Where do babies come from?" I can take a swing at those but like "Why don't I have a dad?" and "Tell me about God." and "When can I have a cell phone?" How do I answer those?

I'm navigating blind. I'm raising her in a world I hardly comprehend and for a future, I can only guess at...

I don't feel qualified to be a mom, yet I am a great mom anyway. I have no handbook and the future is a mystery.

SYMBIOTIC RELATIONSHIP

Tonight, in passing, my eight-year-old daughter gave me an image: She said, "You're like the stick. And I'm like the vine." That's all she said. I am not sure what she was seeing or referencing at that moment, but dang! It spoke volumes to me. When I didn't know what to write for this chapter and how to tackle this question of Motherland, she effortlessly gave me this image.

I am the stick and she is the vine.
Like the prop for my morning glories, I stand strong so she
    can circle, follow the sun,
Climb higher and bloom.

She curls up with me and says, "Snuggling with you is still my favorite thing." Words I will cherish forever. They are even more poignant knowing that, in a few years, that will be the farthest from her sentiment.

She is confident and tender.
Quick to be silly and quick to be hurt.
She's willing to receive a hug when that's all she needs.
She can tell me where and why she's hurt with such
    eloquence and clarity.

It's overwhelming to be a parent. And it's exhilarating.

It is constant. ...and the rewards are many.

Parenting is not a nine-to-five. You don't clock out when they're eighteen. I'm 45 and I still need my parents. We all need parents whether or not we're lucky enough to have them or have their support throughout our lives. This job of caring, supporting, and guiding never ends, even when we don't know what the hell we're doing.

I'M THE PARENT.

I'm the stick she gets to twine around but the lessons I learn from this impossible journey, attempting and failing in countless ways, the lessons I learn from her are infinite.

When we think being an adult or being a parent is the ultimate goal, we forget what our children still have to teach us. While financial literacy, chewing your food, and saying thank you may be important, life, fully living is so much more than showing up on time.

The lessons I learned from my daughter feel more essential to my humanity:

- her ability to be upset
- her courage to show her feelings
- her willingness to forgive
- her ability to laugh
- and her sense of self enough to ask for what she desires

are all lessons that I still aspire to learn and emulate.

- I can make a chore chart and teach her how to wash the dishes
- I can show her how to make cookies and take the dog for a walk
- I can even teach her about compounding interest.

But being a parent is as much about learning as it is about teaching. Together we are each learning to be human and be ourselves.

HOW DO I TEACH A GIRL TO BE A WOMAN OR JUST HERSELF?

I am hardly able to answer that question for myself. What if it's not about having the answers and more about letting her see me trying to figure it out on my own while letting her see where I don't always make the mark?

I set myself such a high bar it's impossible to succeed. But recently I've changed the tune. "At least we're not doing heroin together." We stay up late watching movies, drinking coffee, and generally hanging out. It was the Christmas holiday for god's sake. What did I think was going to happen? A lifetime's worth of core childhood memories, that's what. Hundreds of bonding and foundational moments.

Maybe I set the bar too high... You know what? She's watching. No matter what I do... When I set impossible goals and berate myself. She's watching. When I don't make time for myself and when I work too late and too hard. I'm teaching my child *most* even when I think she's not watching, not just when I'm trying. Some of the things I'm focused on now and working so hard to offer, she won't ever notice or remember. But I'll try anyway. The lessons she learns may well not be the ones I want her to know.

That is a startling realization: that in all the effort, I may be teaching her the opposite lesson I believe in my heart.

I don't know how to do this, but again it is not about getting it right. It is about trying– and here, the best I can do is more about me than her.

WHERE THE ROLE OF MOTHER AND THE IDENTITY OF MOTHER INTERSECT

As the flowers that bloom on the vine that wraps around this stick,
I want to bloom and blossom myself.
Why does that feel so (radical, selfish, grasping, impossible)?

THE JOB OF BEING A MOM

I bought a Bucketlist notebook. For many months it sat empty next to my bed.

I felt wholly incapable of having even one desire or goal for my own life. It was taking all I had at the time just to keep working and caring for my kid. But piece by piece, with attention and focus, I've also been able to carve out little moments for myself.

The role of mother can be eclipsing. It blocks out the sun and has its own gravitational force. It is not the fullness of who I am, yet still, in this phase of life, where she needs so much from me, she is the central figure, the person I factor most significantly into every thought and decision I make. It's no wonder women get lost in the role and identity of motherhood. It requires so much.

How do we continue to exist outside of the role & identity?

Separately strong enough for our children to grow up and around us. Allowing them to grow beyond and not get lost in the gravitational pull of the endless responsibility.

I am making exploratory jaunts to rediscover and reassert who I am. Mom is a central part of who I am. Part of what I can teach her is how to be myself without getting swallowed up into any one role or identity (parent/ publisher/ etc). Our roles and responsibilities take up so much of who we are... but I am more than these things... and allowing her to witness the reassertion of my desires & my identity outside of my responsibilities may be the greatest gift I can give her.

What if being a good mom - today - means just fully being myself and letting her see me try even when I don't know how?

A BOOK IS LIKE A BABY IN SO MANY WAYS.

Why I love writing & publishing.

In addition to momming this incredible young human, I run Red Thread Publishing. **Red Thread Books** was founded with a mission to support 10,000 **women** to become successful published authorpreneurs & thought leaders. We have expanded to incorporate a second imprint [**Red Falcon Press**] for all genders encouraging more silenced and marginalized folks to share their voices & stories.

As we support people to write and publish their stories, we always say that a book is like a baby. The challenges and the rewards of writing match those of parenting. It is an endlessly apt metaphor.

PREGNANT WITH A STORY

- We believe we are in control and guiding the story.
- But the story that wants to be told is coming through regardless.
- Carry a story around with you inside, sometimes for years.
- Birth pushes through the pain & fear to do a truly impossible thing...
- Thank you for holding this fragile little gift.
- It still needs so much from you, your newborn book baby
- To grow to fruition it needs lots of care and attention.

We can get stuck in writing, like in parenting, by having impossibly high or rigid expectations. We may believe this is how we excel, but in reality, it stunts our growth and warps our young creation.

THIS CHAPTER MAY BE A LOVE LETTER TO MY DAUGHTER.

We stayed up too late watching movies tonight *again* and she's gently sleeping next to me. Someday she will read this and get another glimpse or a different understanding of who her mother is. I'm just a girl trying to figure out how to be myself. Actually, with her by my side, I've learned what's worth fighting for.

I'm also discovering parts of myself that never existed before and were not supported to thrive.

It is like an infinity loop
She requires so much
She gives so much in return.
My little tendril vine
May you grow strong, bloom more often
and reach for the sun.
May the seeds you sow
Reach many
and brighten the world.

About the Author

Best-selling author, international speaker & educator, Sierra Melcher is founder of *Red Thread Publishing LLC.* She leads an all-female publishing company, with a mission to support 10,000 women to become successful published authors & thought-leaders. Offering world-class coaching & courses that focus on community, collaboration, and a uniquely feminine approach at every stage of the author process.

Sierra has a Master's degree in education, has spoken & taught around the world. Originally from the United States, Sierra lives in Medellin, Colombia with her young daughter.

instagram.com/redthreadbooks
linkedin.com/in/sierra-melcher
amazon.com/author/sierramelcher
goodreads.com/sierra-melcher

Thank You

If you have enjoyed or found value in this book, please take a moment to leave an honest/brief review on Amazon amzn.to/4cEZotf or Goodreads. Your reviews help prospective readers decide if this is right for them & it is the greatest kindness you can offer the authors.

Thank you in advance.

Acknowledgments

This book is the result of countless mothering moments. It is the culmination of our own dreams and the learning from our own struggles. It is in this process of writing that we both share our vulnerable selves and offer a gift for the readers.

In particular we want to thank our author mentors, who have supported all contributing writers:

- Frances D. Trejo-Lay
- Jessical Goldmutz Stokes
- Erika Hull

These women have shared, coached and guided the contributors through the technical, logistical and emotional journey that is writing and becoming an author.

Thanks to all who have led us to this moment. May it ripple.

Other Red Thread Books

OUR BOOKS ABOUT WRITING & PUBLISHING:

The Anatomy of a Book: 21 Book Experts Share What Aspiring Authors
Need to Know About Writing, Publishing & Book Marketing

Typo: The Art of Imperfect Creation, *Permission to Do it Badly*

Story Ink: *A Cyclical Methodology to Write 1 or 100 Books* (2024)

Write: *An Interactive Guide to Drafting Your Manuscript* (forthcoming)

TO SEE ALL OUR PUBLISHED WORKS VISIT OUR LIBRARY:

bit.ly/RedThreadLibrary

PREVIOUS COLLABORATIVE TITLES IN THE BRAVE NEW VOICES SERIES:

Planting the Seed:

Feisty: *Dangerously Amazing Women Using Their Voices & Making An Impact*

Spark: *Women in the Business of Changing the World* - 1 sentence description

Sanctuary: *Cultivating Safe Space in Sisterhood; Rediscovering the Power that Unites Us*

Planting the Seed: Lessons to Cultivate a Brighter Future

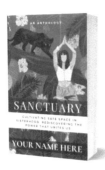

**Sisterhood Redefines Us
(Collaborative)**

We are stronger together, but we must find or create our own safety first. (10 authors)

Dangerously Amazing Women (Collaborative)

If you're ready to rewrite all the rules & start thriving, just as you are, then Feisty is a must-read! (19 authors)

Women In the Business of Changing the World (Collaborative)

Celebrating the extraordinary impact of ordinary women, women when we show up & shine in our full, unapologetic authority. (10 authors)

WRITE & PUBLISH WITH US AS A COLLABORATIVE AUTHOR

Be the next **Red Thread Collaborative Author:** bit.ly/46Yd6Ed

Well we are an on-purpose, for-profit company, driven by a powerful mission. It costs money to produce a great book but we acknowledge that not every voice is bankrolled. We believe every story matters, not just the stories of the women who can afford to publish them. Therefore we have built-in to our business structure scholarship funds using profits to support organizations for good in the world as well as our first-time authors anthology publishing

Access our Free Author Resources

bit.ly/RedThreadResources

Red Thread Publishing

Red Thread Publishing is an all-female publishing company on a mission to support 10,000 women to become successful published authorpreneurs & thought leaders.

To work with us or connect regarding any of our growing library of books email us at **info@redthreadbooks.com** .

To learn more about us visit our website **www.redthreadbooks.com**.

Follow us & join the community.

facebook.com/redthreadpublishing
instagram.com/redthreadbooks

Made in United States
Troutdale, OR
04/23/2024

19384495R00105